The DO or
DIE
ENTREPRENEUR

© 2004 by Young Paik
Published by Random House JoongAng Inc.,

Printed in KOREA
Random House JoongAng Inc.,
6th Fl., PaiChai Bldg., B. #34-5, Jeong-dong,
Joong-ku, Seoul, 100-120, Korea
tel 82-2-3705-0119   fax 82-2-3705-0111

ISBN 89-5757-926-5

THE DO OR DIE

ENTREPRENEUR

BY YOUNG PAIK WITH JOHN CHA

RANDOM HOUSE JOONGANG

CONTENTS

INTRODUCTION • 6

Chapter 1 STEEL MAGIC_11

Chapter 2 CHESTNUT GROVE_22

Chapter 3 REFUGEE_42

Chapter 4 CHESTNUT VENDOR_55

Chapter 5 HUNG SA DAHN_64

Chapter 6 FOREIGNER_79

Chapter 7 FOREIGN STUDENT_89

Chapter 8 INDIANA BOUND_108

Chapter 9 INTERN_123

Chapter 10 ENGINEER_133

Chapter 11 SALES ENGINEER_143

Chapter 12 ON MY OWN_153

Chapter 13 PACO_161

Chapter 14 CUSTOMER IS KING_174

Chapter 15 SUMITOMO STEEL_183

Chapter 16 CORRUGATED BEAM_189

Chapter 17 TRIALS AND TRIBULATIONS_199

Chapter 18 THE ROAD BACK_205

Chapter 19 NEGOTIATING FOR LTV_208

Chapter 20 MOTHER_220

Chapter 21 PYONGYANG
 –DIFFERENT PLACE, DIFFERENT TIME_234

Chapter 22 ECONOMIC DELEGATION_245

Chapter 23 HWANG JANG-YOP_262

Chapter 24 MOTHER'S TEARS_270

Chapter 25 ARKANSAS PLANT_279

Chapter 26 ENTREPRENEUR OF THE YEAR_283

Chapter 27 YENZI_289

EPILOG • 306

INTRODUCTION

It is no coincidence that I met Mr. Young Paik through Mrs. Susan Ahn Cuddy. I had written a book on Susan Ahn Cuddy, and when she introduced me to Young Paik at a restaurant in Los Angeles several years ago, I was struck by his genteel, candid demeanor, not at all the picture of a steel tycoon that I had drawn in my mind. It didn't take me long to find out what was behind his quiet politeness: an unbending will and the confidence to go with it.

Susan Ahn Cuddy and Young Paik go back a long way. Born in Los Angeles in 1915, Susan Ahn Cuddy is a daughter of Dosan Ahn Chang-Ho, a revered patriot and philosopher. Dosan had come to America from Korea in 1902 and as one of his many achievements formed an organization called Hung Sa Dahn (Young Korean Academy) in San Francisco in 1913. Hung Sa Dahn was the organization that sponsored Young Paik's journey to America in 1956.

Dosan had long since passed away by then, dying in a Japanese prison in 1938. Although Young Paik never met Dosan, he is devoted to Dosan and his teachings. One of

Dosan's teachings, "Never tell a lie...even in death," is a guiding principle for Young Paik, and has been throughout his life.

What I find remarkable is Young Paik's dedication to honesty, and this integrity is the same quality I see in Susan Ahn Cuddy. No doubt they are connected through Dosan, and I feel forever honored to have come to know these historic individuals and to write about them.

As I said, it is no coincidence that I met Young Paik through Susan Ahn Cuddy. As a transplant to America myself at an early age, I was meant to tell their stories as part of my lifelong quest to unravel what's behind the Korean question, our sense of self, culture, and country.

My good friend and mentor Elaine Kim at UC Berkeley said, "History is a very personal thing with me." She has family members scattered throughout in China, Japan, Korea, and America speaking different languages, unable to communicate with each other. For those who otherwise would have lived as one family in Korea in peace, they have been relegated to travel separate ways. Trying to understand how they got there is a historical lesson in itself.

To know who we are and what we are, we need to understand how our lives are so intricately intertwined with the global events. I see Susan's story as one that takes us back to the final days of Yi Dynasty, the Japanese colonization of Korea, World War II, and the liberation that came with the conclusion of the Great War.

Young Paik's story takes us to the next major event in our lives–the Korean War. He lived in the middle of it, spent his poverty-stricken days as a lonely young man from North Korea. We see him struggling as a student in America; we see him struggling and fighting his way to becoming a successful businessman; and finally receiving the coveted Entrepreneur of the Year Award.

Such extraordinary achievement by a man who started with nothing smacks of Horatio Alger and all the American tales of rags to riches, and like Horatio Alger, Young Paik's American dream came true for him.

However, his story doesn't end there. Young Paik has yet to fulfill another dream that awaits him at the other side of a world called North Korea, where his brother is reportedly living in a concentration camp. He dreams about seeing his younger brother again, yet this is one dream he can't seem to do anything about. He can only hope that all the ongoing talks surrounding the Korean peninsula come to a successful conclusion so that people, families can travel freely.

Young Paik is just one of the million plus families who have been separated for more that fifty years now, many of whom have perished without knowing the fate of their loved ones. For those who are still alive, they are barely hanging on, wondering how much longer the madness will continue.

I am truly grateful that Mr. Young Paik has made his story available for all of us to share.

John Cha
November, 2004

chapter 1

STEEL MAGIC

Welding spatter, thick smoke, hammers banging on steel: these are the sights and sounds that I grew to love. Add the acrid smell of smoke from burning welding rods into the mix, I am at home when I enter a steel fabrication shop, be it in Savannah, Georgia or in Tacoma, Washington. A large steel plant or a small shop, I feel like a child in a candy store and I forget about everything else, who I am, where I am. As I said, I am at home in a steel fabrication shop, far more comfortable than in an easy chair in my living room. I suppose an equestrian feels the same kind of excitement when he or she enters a barn filled with fine horses.

You may ask how anyone can get so excited about burning welding rods, the blue arc that can blind your eyes without a shield. Borrow a shield some time, and look through the black glass at a welder weaving a bright molten pool between two pieces of metal. I guarantee that you will feel the magic of steels coming together as one. You will see what I am talking about, the electricity, the heat. Remember to cover your nose and mouth with something, a mask or a cloth, so you don't breathe the fume from the flux—magnesium gas—that protects the molten pool from oxygen. If the oxygen in the air makes contact with the molten pool, it will rust and make slag; slag is something welders avoid like a plague because it weakens the joint.

THE DO OR DIE ENTREPRENEUR

I make and sell steel beams for a living. Tons and tons of them. My company ships about 300,000 tons of steel beams a year to all corners of the continental U.S., and I have been doing it since the mid-1970s. That is a lot of beams to deal with, especially for a small, skinny guy like me. I stand at 5 feet 4 inches tall and weigh 140 pounds.

Why so many beams and what do they do with them? Well, beams in general hold up things like floors and truck beds. For regular house construction one uses 2-by-8 or 2-by-10 wood beams, that is, 2 inches wide and 8 or 10 inches deep when you look at the ends of the beams. For truck beds they use steel beams, and when you look at the end of a steel beam, you see the shape of an "I." You see two flat pieces, one at the top and the other at the bottom. These flat pieces are called flanges, top flange and bottom flange. The upright piece in between the top and bottom flanges is called the web. Because of its "I" shape, the steel beam is called "I-beam," a term that I will be using quite a bit.

Now I didn't grow up thinking about I-beams. I learned about I-beams when I went to Indiana Institute of Technology in Fort Wayne, Indiana, where I earned an engineering degree back in 1959. It wasn't until I began working for Soule (pronounced, shu-lay) Steel Company in southern

California that I became interested in steel fabrication, the sparks, the fumes. How exciting it was to see pieces of steel transform into real things like buildings, factories, bridges, water tanks, and trucks.

In school, an I-beam was merely a diagram, a line drawn on a flat piece of paper, without weight or feel to it. Take a ten foot long I-beam with 8-inch depth, for example. If it fell on you it could crush you because it weighs somewhere between 200 pounds to 1,000 pounds, depending on how thick the plates are, the flange plates and the web plates. But then you need to simplify things to the level of stick diagrams and mockups to test various theories and learn to analyze different situations. That's what school is for: to learn theories and principles through books and experimentation. I am glad that I have had the college training, which gave me the fundamental knowledge for my invention later.

As I said, however, the physical reality of steelworks was so different that it excited me like never before. People wanted me to design real roof trusses, not a hypothetical situation someone had crafted for an exercise in a book. And they wanted it NOW. I mean, right now. The foundation was already set in place, they hollered, and they were waiting on Soule to set the columns and the roof trusses. Soule was getting a lot of money to design the real structure, to fabricate it with real I-beams, angle irons and plates, and to deliver it. We had jobs all over California and the western States, and I was pumped up. I woke up early every morning at the crack of dawn, already thinking about the piles of drawings awaiting me in my office, and the structures taking shape in the noisy shop. I would gulp down tea, toast and eggs my wife made for me every morning and dash out of the house like a man possessed. Every morning, she would say, "Have a nice day," and like a good Korean husband, I would wave my hand and grunt as I went out the door.

Now some people may ask, "What kind of person just grunts at his wife as he goes out the door?" Frankly, I don't know how I got away with grunts like that, especially when we were just starting out as a family. Somehow I think Korean husbands are supposed to be preoccupied, constantly thinking about work and the problems of the world. I certainly was preoccupied with my job at Soule, and my wife did her best to keep me away from any distraction. Between the two of us, I am glad to say that she is the manager of our lives, and in her scheme of things, my job was to concentrate on my job only. She took care of all the financial chores, thank goodness, for I was not very good with money. In fact, I did not pay any attention to my salary, nor did I know what other engineers were making. Soule paid me what I presumed to be a good salary, and I brought home the paychecks and gave them to my wife for her to do whatever she did with them. Our roles were clear and simple, and we were both comfortable with our respective roles. I suppose couples nowadays do things differently, and they would consider our arrangement strange and maybe even old-fashioned, but it worked out well for us through the good times and bad.

I met Kyung-sook Yang in 1960 when she was a graduate student in Chicago, and the prettiest girl there. I was out of I.I.T. (Indiana Institute of Technology) then, interning as an engineer-in-training at Van Wert County, located in the western part of Ohio between Toledo and Cincinnati. I liked the people in rural Ohio who were quiet and nice, and especially the Chief Engineer who hired me at the recommendation of my professor at I.I.T. But I was lonely there, being the only Korean for miles around. And I missed rice terribly. The only rice the town store carried was the long grained rice from Louisiana or Texas, which had the familiar grainy quality but not the taste or the consistency. Nevertheless, I boiled the long grained rice in a pot in the evenings. For a side dish I peeled an onion and sliced it and sprinkled red hot Tabasco sauce all over the onion slices, a bachelor's rendition of kimchi, the pickled cabbage. Another specialty of mine was mixed tomato catsup with red pepper powder, pretending that it was *gochoojahng*, the hot bean paste from home. Well, none of my concoctions was anywhere near the real thing, but the hot rice and the crunchy onion burned my tongue and inside of my mouth just the same. But then you can go only so far with makeshift imitations.

When I heard of a Korean church in Chicago where a handful of Korean students gathered regularly, I bought my first car, a brand new 1960 Chevy Belair, and I drove to Chicago about two hours away. I was a happy guy, tooling down on Highway 30 west through Fort Wayne, Indiana, then Gary, and on to Chicago. My anticipation grew as I got closer to the Loop.

As it turned out, the folks at the Methodist church, about three hundred of them, were much better off than I was. Chicago offered a better selection of vegetables and sundries for them to make real Korean dishes. I was able to get bean sprouts, tofu, sautéed spinach, even real kimchi, and I thought I was in heaven. After the Sunday service by Reverend Eun-taek Lee, people brought out potluck dishes on a long table, and enjoyed a feast of a lifetime. I attacked the banquet with gusto, helping myself to heaping portions of food I had not seen for several years. Table manners were not on my mind as I went for second and third servings. No doubt that people snickered as they watched me wolf down the food, but I didn't care. There were other young men just as hungry as I was, and together we must have made quite a scene. No matter, I decided then I would return the following weekend and I did.

I looked forward to Fridays. "TGIF" had a new meaning for me because at five o'clock on Friday I was on the road to Chicago, my newly found home. I made sure that I finished all my work on time and cleaned my desk and my drafting board before I ran out the door. Everyone in the office knew where I was going, and they didn't have to ask. And no one minded that I kept my eye on the clock as quitting time came closer because come five o'clock, I had already put in nine or ten hours of work.

I was an early riser, a habit I picked up when I was a busboy in Los Angeles back in 1956, a habit that stayed with me throughout my life. I like the feel of coming dawn, the quiet anticipation of a new day. I like being there waiting for the daybreak before it comes. But then I had nothing else to do after showering, shaving, cleaning and dressing. So I went to work. I was at work two hours ahead of everyone else, and by the time they showed up, I was well into my chores, filing and working on as-built drawings for the steel structures, bridges and buildings. As an intern, I was at the bottom of the totem pole. I ended up with all the "boring" tasks of record keeping while other engineers busied themselves with planning new roads and new developments, but I didn't mind so-called the "shit jobs" at all. Besides the early rising habit, I had learned as a busboy that there was no menial task, and that people respected hard work no matter what the task was. I made up for my limited English with hard work and hustle, so my superiors did not mind my frequent glimpses at the clock come five on Fridays.

A week or two later I met Kyung-sook. She was one of ten or so girls who went to school in Chicago, and got a lot of attention from the 200 or so male students scattered about the Chicago area. The majority of men were studying for their Masters or Doctorates, barely making it with the money sent from home and the part time jobs at restaurants. And there I was, a new guy in town with a real job, extra money and a bright blue Chevy. The other fellows must have hated me when I offered to buy *mahndu* dumplings for the girls one day. The girls perked up immediately.

"*Mahndu?* Where did you find *mahndu?*" One girl clamored.

Another girl chimed, "Oh, *mahndu*, I haven't had *mahndu* ever since I left home. My mother made the best *mahndu* in the world. I used to help her roll the fresh dough. She made it so thin and chewy. You take some of mom's filling and make a ball and wrap it in the dough skin and fold and crimp the edges like so and like so. We'd boil them, steam them and fry them, and eat them until our stomachs blew up. Mom's special sauce for New Year's day! Mmm. What I would give for one of those dumplings, to dip it in the sauce and bite into the bits of meat, tofu, kimchi, rice noodle, oh, and what else did she put in, eggs, and, and..."

"I'm hungry," the first girl said, "Mr. Paik, can we all go?"

I nodded confidently, and they piled in the car. I took them to a Chinese restaurant and ordered wonton dumpling soup for everyone. When the soup came, the girls protested, "Mr. Paik, this is not *mahndu*, but it's good." Another girl said, "Mr. Paik tricked us," and we laughed heartily as we slurped the soup and ate the "Chinese *mahndu*."

I don't recall if Kyung-sook came with me to the *mahndu* outing. She thought I was brash at first. We were polite to each other when we met at the church, saying hello in the hallways as we passed each other, and that was all.

I don't remember exactly when I began calling her "Sue," her American name, which was a lot easier to say than "Miss Yang," or "Kyung-sook-ssi," an honorific that came with a certain degree of familiarity while maintaining a certain degree of respectfulness. The American way of addressing each other is a lot easier and simpler than the complicated Korean system, and I began calling her Sue, and she called me Young.

Today, Sue says, "There were a lot of Korean men around Chicago at that time. A lot them. Of all of them, Young impressed me the most. He seemed so honest and intelligent. And he touched my heart as no one could. I felt like I had to help him."

We liked driving out to Lakeshore Drive and walking around the park on Lake Michigan. So huge and peaceful, the lake invited us to bare our souls to each other, reminiscing about our childhood back in Korea and sharing our dreams about the future. She liked what she saw in me, even though I was alone in this world without a father, and without knowing the fate of my mother, my younger brothers and sisters in North Korea. If they were even still alive.

chapter 2

CHESTNUT GROVE

Sue was a good listener, thank God. For hours I would go on a long narrative binge, with her pretty eyes fixed on me. She didn't know then that she was talking to a young man she would later accompany to receive "The Entrepreneur of the Year (EOY)" Award. Nor did I know that the same award would go to the likes of Bill Gates and Ted Turner. In terms of American life I was four years old and she was one, and we knew very little about America, let alone the EOY.

During the Lakeshore Drive days we didn't talk too much about what was going on around us at the time, the Kennedy-Nixon debates and the presidential campaign that charged everyone up. Elvis Presley didn't do much for me, nor did the rest of the rock-n-rollers. Frankly, we didn't have the wherewithal or the time to understand new fads and new attitudes emerging at that time. We had our own world to deal with, the world that was first shaped by the Japanese rule in Korea, then the liberation, followed by the Korean War and its aftermath.

Sue was fascinated with my childhood stories, where I was born, where and how I grew up. I told Sue about my life in a tiny village called Moon Heung Li in Sungchun township, about 25 miles north of Pyongyang. Our village was snuggled in a small valley affectionately called "Chestnut Grove," because of the countless chestnut trees that lined the surrounding hills and the mountains. Chestnut Grove is a master's painting in my mind, its colors so vivid and pleasant, still as clear today as it was then. In my mind the clear spring water in front of the house is as fresh and ice-cold as it was then. And there was the stone Buddha figurine up the hill, the gentle hill we called "Front Mountain." The Buddha was my friend, although he was not the best looking fellow, his features rather crude and scarred. I never considered him ugly, however, because his rounded features struck me as kind and genuine. I saw him everyday and said hello on my six-mile walk to grade school, up and down hills and along the river.

I had a job, too. My father had me feed the orange ox

every day, a two-hour chore that I remember as the most peaceful time of my life. I see myself in that master's painting far away, a boy without a care, following the bovine critter from one clump of grass to another. On rainy days or in the winter, I fed him hay in the barn at the back of the house, and on dry days I let him graze around the Front Mountain. Watching him chew grass was not all that exciting, and I'd lie down and watch the clouds and fall asleep sometimes. I'd wake up and see that he had chewed his way down a few yards ahead and I'd follow him. Then I'd fall asleep again, and he'd move ahead while I dozed. He fed for two hours or so and when his belly stretched and ballooned rock hard, it was time for him to take a nap. I didn't know how good I had it at the time, and that I would take these moments with me into adulthood. Even now, some sixty years later, I cherish the memory of those carefree days in Chestnut Grove, those sweet apples, pears, persimmons, and especially chestnuts hanging from the trees that my father and one of my uncles had planted in back of the house.

Father was a good farmer, and we never went hungry. Even though he was just a sharecropper, he worked the small farm as if it was his own, bringing a good harvest every year. We had plenty of millet grains, wheat and corn for the long winter months, and enough cabbage for the winter kimchi. Mother prepared every day my bento (which means lunch box in Japanese), packing a metal box full with rice. For relish she put in kimchi or *gochujahng*. For a kid, lunchtime should have been the best part of the day. But I dreaded taking out my tin-colored bento and placing it on my desk while other kids brought out their shiny, sleek lunch boxes made out of aluminum. I don't know why those anodized aluminum lunch containers looked so much better than my beat-up box. I was even ashamed of my lunch which was rice and kimchi only, and I wolfed it down as quickly as possible. I didn't want the girls to tease me like they usually did about my lunch while they were chewing pieces of *jahngjorim*, stringy beef chunks poached in soy sauce, and other delicacies. I didn't like those giggly girls and I couldn't wait till the classes restarted. The classroom was where I shined, especially when test scores were announced. Their fancy lunch boxes didn't mean anything then because I had the top score. Always. Year after year. Still, I wished that mother would make me a lunch like theirs just once. She simply couldn't afford to buy the expensive ingredients, and I didn't understand that simple fact.

I never thought of myself as poor, though, and Chestnut Grove holds my happiest childhood memories. But I knew that I would leave the village some day. I wanted to go out into the world to see big cities and do big things. I did not want to stay in a small farming village and follow my father's footsteps. My father felt the same way, that I was destined for bigger and better things. He was an intelligent, self-educated man, the only one who could read and write in the village. But he didn't get very far in terms of formal education because he had refused to learn the Japanese language. Japanese was the official language at that time and all the schools taught in Japanese. A fierce Korean patriot, he wouldn't learn or speak Japanese. He never regretted his decision, however, and he had high hopes for me. He studied mathematics, language and science with me night after night. He told me that I had to go to Pyongyang Teacher's College, a tuition-free school, because he couldn't support me through the regular school.

At school, all my teachers were Japanese until I was fifteen years old, and there were strict rules against speaking or reading Korean. Those who were caught for speaking Korean were punished with cleaning chores or whipping, or both. On August 15, 1945, all the Japanese teachers were gone.

Yes, August 15 was a memorable day, the day I listened to Emperor Hirohito's high pitched voice on the radio, the surrendering speech. He spoke in a halting voice, "After pondering deeply the general trends of the world Our Empire accepts the provisions of their Joint Declaration." I had no idea what Hirohito was talking about. I didn't know that he was referring to the Potsdam Declaration by the Allied Powers. The more I listened, the more anxious I became. All I wanted to know was that Japan had lost the war, but he didn't mention it. I kept listening. "To strive for the common prosperity and happiness of all nations as well as the security and well being of Our subjects is the solemn obligation which has been handed down by Our Imperial Ancestors, which we lay close to heart. Indeed, We declared war on America and Britain out of Our sincere desire to ensure Japan's self preservation and the stabilization of East Asia, it being far from Our thought either to infringe upon the sovereignty of other nations or to embark upon territorial aggrandizement."

My ears were glued to the radio, but I didn't understand any of the words at the time. I kept listening for the simple words *We surrender*. The special broadcast continued, "Despite the best that has been done by everyone—gallant fighting of military and Naval forces, the diligence and assiduity of Our servants of the State and the devoted service of Our one hundred million people, the war situation has not necessarily improved, and the general trends of the world are also not to Japan's advantage."

The emperor went on without saying the word "surrender," and I wasn't sure if the war was over. Outside, many people crowded the street, waving hundreds of Tae Geuk flags, the Korean national flags, in frenzied euphoria, yelling about liberation and independence. I was convinced that Japan was defeated then, and joined in the celebration, running and jumping around all over Sungchun town the whole day.

If I had strutted around the streets with a Tae Geuk flag in my hand the day before, I would have been arrested. Independence was a good thing.

With the liberation came new teachers, all Koreans, and we spoke Korean in classrooms. At times though, when teachers called on me to answer questions, Japanese words blurted out of me. My classmates laughed, and I laughed. The teacher scolded me for speaking Japanese, but the scolding didn't bother me. I was happy.

When I told Sue about this, she laughed and laughed,

recalling her own experiences as a youngster in school, having to switch gears overnight from Japanese to Korean. "Those crazy days…" We sighed simultaneously after each story and looked out to the endless Lake Michigan, awash with so many stories, sad stories, funny stories. It was a huge lake, stretching for miles and miles as far as we could see and beyond, and we gave it our precious memories from the other side of the world.

With the liberation, our hopes soared for better days along with the rest of the country. The euphoria didn't last long, however. The country was split into two parts by that invisible line called the 38th parallel, an arbitrary line devised to accept the Japanese surrender in the peninsula. The Russians were to supervise the process of surrendering in the regions north of the line, and the Americans in the south. Once the Japanese surrender was completed, the line was supposed to finish its role. Contrary to our expectation, however, the line became a permanent one. Because my home was near Pyongyang, north of the 38th parallel, I found myself saluting to a strange flag with a red star and listening to Kim Il Sung's speeches and Marxist slogans. The Tae Geuk flag disappeared out of sight. What happened to it, I wondered.

My father, bless his soul, didn't approve of communism. He respected men like Ahn Chang Ho and Cho Man Shik instead, and he always talked about them. Dosan Ahn Chang Ho passed away when I was eight years old and I only knew him through my father as the man who built schools in Pyongyang and who devoted his life to the independence of Korea. Dosan had gone to America and then went to work for the Korean Provisional Government in Shanghai, my father told me. Like Ahn Chang Ho, Cho Man Shik was a democratic leader who struggled against the Japanese. My father didn't think much about Kim Il Sung, but he had no choice but to go along with the new government. Dissatisfaction with the new government started with the new taxation, which required him to give up 30% of the crop. He obliged. But later the officials came back for more with a written quota. The quota had no relation to the size of the crop, but they badgered my father to rescind. They said to my father, "We know you've hidden away a lot. You should give more."

By the time they finished, the taxation tallied up to 80% of the crop, and my father raised his voice to the communist party officials. "You told me 30% to begin with. How can you take 80% of the crop? This way, my family will starve to death."

Then the party officials shouted at my father, "A traitor like you should be locked up in jail." The threat shocked me, and I thought they were going to haul him off to jail. My father saw that there wasn't anything he could do or say and he kept quiet. After that day he complained about the communists continually.

Then he joined the Democratic Party led by Cho Man Shik, an illegal organization in North Korea, and he attended the meetings and other party activities in secret. As a middle school student, I didn't know enough to ask him questions about what was going on with communism and democracy.

At school I was considered a good public speaker, and my grades were among the top. The school official told me, "You are a good public speaker and a model student. I want you to join the communist party. And later we'll send you to Russia for study if you want."

Hearing this, my father sighed and said firmly, "My son, do not join the communist party. And never go to Russia to study, absolutely not. Russia… it's a bad country, which is run by bad people, and they will perish and fail soon. So never mind about joining the party and going to Russia no matter what they say."

I believed my father, even though I envied some of my friends who were selected for the elite opportunity to study abroad in Moscow. I didn't join the party because of what my father told me. All the while though, I thought my father was mistaken about Russia and I felt unhappy about his advice. I thought that he would have been a wonderful party man because he was intelligent and spoke with authority on matters of politics. I wondered why he hated the communist party so much especially when he was neither wealthy nor a landowner. I resented my father for a long time for taking away the opportunity that my best friends had. My resentment grew more about the time when I was working as a teacher in Pyongyang after graduating from Pyongyang Teacher's College. He practically abandoned his family and he hid at my house while working against the communist party. I thought that he should have stayed with the farm and tended to his responsibility as the head of his family, instead of sneaking around in Pyongyang. Poor mother, I thought, she now had to look after the family.

One day I spoke up about his doings. "Father, why do you oppose the communists so intensely? You shouldn't do that."

Father replied firmly, "If I don't do my work for the country now, when can I do it? What I do is all for the good of the country!"

I saw that he was a determined man with a mission and I wasn't about to persuade him otherwise. I found new respect for my father after that conversation. However, I didn't know how deep his belief was and how far he went in opposing the communists.

On June 25, 1950, the Korean War broke out, and our lives were turned upside down. My father and I left Pyongyang and returned to Chestnut Grove away from the bombing and shooting. The village was quiet and remote from the war itself. We did not hear anything for some months. Then one day, the news came that the United Nations troops and the South Korean divisions were pushing back northward and that they were marching through Pyongyang. My father was the first one to get the news and he exclaimed, "This is the end of communism for our nation!"

He didn't have to stay hidden any longer now as the roles were reversed between the communists and the democracy followers. The communists went underground, and the followers of democracy surfaced as the people of power. My father organized his colleagues from the Democratic Party and spread the news throughout the village, getting ready to welcome the oncoming U.N. and the South Korean troops. He also organized a police force in the name of preserving peace in the village. This was his way of rooting out known communists, his enemies. It was his turn to get back at those who had taken away 80% of his crop in the name of the fatherland. It was his turn to persecute those who had persecuted him and his friends. The communists had taken away not only crops but land from landowners, homes from homeowners, and stripped the villagers of their possessions. The communists did so by holding public trials, calling certain people "the enemy of the fatherland," and throwing them into jail after a circus-like event.

Chestnut Grove was no longer a sleepy village. The village that had endured the Japanese domination together forgot the joy of liberation, the celebration of the Tae Geuk flag. They found enemies amongst themselves. In the name of peace and in the name of the fatherland, my father arrested and shot the communists. His methods weren't as cruel as the communists had been, but nevertheless I became less proud of my father after watching his conduct as the head of the police force. To me, he was no less cruel than the communists in terms of propagating misery within the village I grew up in. War is hell.

Even though I was a twenty-year-old teacher then, I didn't really understand what was happening to me, my family and the villagers. In the end the villagers were suffering the most, forced to choose one side or the other, communism or democracy, with very little understanding of the principles of either system. It was truly a sad period of time in Chestnut Grove, the painful days I do not care to remember. We were all trapped on a ship in a stormy sea, powerless and rudderless, left only to feel the turbulence all around us.

After a month or so, around November of 1950, the Chinese communists joined the war and the communist forces were pushing the U.N. and the South Korean armies southward. The rumor spread that the North Korean army was due in Chestnut Grove in a few days. The villagers who had sided with the democratic party readied themselves to escape the village and the inevitable repercussion from the communists. My father and the hardcore band of forty or so refused to leave the village. The leader of the group, my father stood his ground saying, "Let's guard the village with guns."

The village guardsmen took their positions on the hills surrounding the village. The villagers roasted chestnuts and

took them up to the hill for the guardsmen. I didn't participate in the guardsmen's activities. I wanted to stay back and
look after my mother and my younger siblings. At that time
my uncles and aunts were staying with us, away from
Pyongyang, and my mother and I were busy taking care of
all the relatives and the children. My father came down from
the hill during the day and went back up to the hill by
night.

Then one day, on November 22nd as I recall, the sounds
of exploding guns rocked the village at dawn. The North
Korean army had entered the village. Hearing the guns, the
guardsmen up in the hill responded with their own rifles.
The North Korean soldiers stopped shooting as though they
were studying where the guardsmen were located. It
seemed that the North Korean soldiers were deliberate in
shooting and advancing towards the village while the
guardsmen aimed and shot wildly. The guardsmen ran out
of ammunition eventually and they began abandoning their
posts one by one. I was worried about my father and I went
up to the front mountain to study the situation. From the
front mountain, I could see that the northern troops were
about to overrun the village. I needed to get away myself.
Right then my younger brother, Young-ik, ran up after me.

"*Hyung*, my older brother, I'm here."

I saw that he had rushed up the hill in bare feet. Apparently he saw me leaving the house and he figured that I was leaving the village and he wanted to come with me wherever I was going.

"What about mother and the kids?" I asked. I was worried about the family. Also, he was barefooted and he wasn't ready to go anywhere on the frozen grounds.

"If you come with me, what will happen to mother and the small ones? Go back and hide out for three or four days. When the American troops return I'll come back right away. Be patient and wait till then," I told my younger brother. I thought that my brother would be safe at home because he was still a youngster, whereas I was definitely a target for the communist soldiers.

"Okay, I'll do what you say," Young-ik nodded weakly and turned around. I watched him shuffle his bare feet down the hill, his head hanging low between his slumped shoulders.

That was the last time I saw him.

After Young-ik left, I went up a little further for a better vantage-point. Suddenly, guns exploded all around me, piercing my ears. Then my father and several armed men rushed out of the forest. It was about five in the morning, near dawn. They had come to the front mountain to check up on the family. Right at that instant, the Northern (People's Army) soldiers charged the hill, yelling "Yaaah!" in unison.

Someone in the group yelled, "Run!"

All of us ran out of there. I ran and ran like a madman. I don't know how long I ran but I looked around and I didn't see my father in the group any longer. We ran further up toward the top of the mountain, thinking that we should go over the mountain to Sungchun and then on to Pyongyang. Someone said that the Northern soldiers had already taken the mountaintop and that it was dangerous to continue south toward Sungchun. The group headed north. We traveled north for quite a while, and during the process, I found myself alone. I figured that I should go somewhere I was familiar with and I doubled back down to Sungchun where my old high school was located. But the situation was about the same there. Southern soldiers were retreating along with the U.N. troops. As soon as I entered the town I learned that my younger cousin, Young-ryul, had been shot to death in a battle against the Northern soldiers. When I heard about his death, I became angry and scared simultaneously. I told myself that I should retrieve his body at least and headed for the battleground. On my way to find Young-ryul's body, a Southern soldier grabbed me and slapped me hard across the face, and yelled, "You dumb bastard, where the hell you think you're going! Go back!"

Other Southern soldiers came and chased me away from there. I turned around to see what was going on, and saw the soldiers were hauling things out of an empty house. Watches, jewelry, and whatever they could carry. They were stealing and they didn't want people to see them.

I headed for Pyongyang. On the way to Pyongyang I decided to check in on my older sister who lived in a village between Sungchun and Pyongyang. I walked on the back roads, away from the main road. I found my way to my sister's and I was happy to see her. I hadn't eaten for a several days, and she made a warm meal for me. I recovered from hunger after a few days. I was thinking about what I should do next when a group of refugees from my hometown stopped by and gave us the shocking news about my father. My father and my uncle had been caught near the village, and the Northern soldiers shot them both to death.

During the wartime you get used to death and destruction. You get numb and almost cavalier about death and dying all around you, but never about your own father. The news took me to a dark place where I literally couldn't see anything. Nothing made sense.

Then anger set in. I became angry with the Northern soldiers. I became angry at the world, the Russians, the Chinese, the Americans, the U.N., the North, the South, and all of Korea. I even resented my father for having failed to live, leaving behind mother and the small ones. Who would take care of them now, and how would they manage?

Were they still alive?

Once I was over the shock of my father's death, I worried over my family's fate, but I couldn't go back just yet. Not while the Northern soldiers and the communist party held the village. All the villagers supporting democracy had left the village or died, and the communists were sure to purge the village of all those who couldn't escape. If I went back, I would have been captured and killed for sure because they would have been watching our house day and night. As far as I knew mother and the little ones were still alive and I told myself that I must stay alive and try to bring my family out of there. I must stay alive, I thought, if I am to have any chance of helping them. Going back then would be suicide. The communist forces were pushing farther south, and I was convinced that I should leave with the U.N. forces and the Southern army. They would regroup and push the communist forces away from my Chestnut Grove like they had done before. I'd come back then.

I talked to my sister about my decision.

"*Noonim,* my older sister, I'm going to head south for a while."

She didn't like the idea. She said, "No place is safe these days. Wouldn't it be better to hide around here for a while?"

I replied, "No, I don't think so. They killed our father. I don't think there's a place for me to hide around here. I'll go south for a while and come back as soon as the crisis calms down."

"Well, it's hard to tell when the crisis will calm down."

I assured her then, "I don't think it'll be very long. The U.N. forces will win the war and let us go back to Chestnut Grove."

chapter 3

REFUGEE

One week, I said, I'd be gone one week at the most before I returned to Chestnut Grove, and I left for Pyongyang. Pyongyang was no longer the beautiful city it once was. The city was in shambles, eerily quiet with signs of destruction everywhere. The U.N. troops were still visible, but I knew the communist forces weren't too far away. So did the thousands of people that filled the streets, the older folks riding ox carts, the little ones strapped on their parents' back, fathers with loads on their backs, mothers with loads on their heads holding their children by the hands. No one said anything. The occasional sounds of canons exploding in the distance signaled the impending doom, and the subdued refugees quickened their paces. When the U.N. trucks or jeeps approached them, they parted without a sound as though they had rehearsed the maneuver.

Through the crowds and over the rubble, I managed to reach my Uncle Je-yong's house, my father's younger brother, and I stayed there overnight. During the night we talked about our southward trek ahead of the retreating U.N. troops. In the morning Uncle Je-yong said he had to take care of some details at the police station where he worked as a policeman and then he and I would embark on our evacuation trip south. He never made it back home, though. I didn't hear from him for a long while and two gentlemen from Chestnut Grove, Lee Dong-ho and Park Dong-sun, and I went on the road to join the melee of refugees. We didn't know where we were going, but we followed the endless stream of people toward south.

We reached Daedong River. What had been a steady stream of people following one after another had come to an end. At the northern shore of the river I saw pandemonium, a massive hysterical mob of people crying, yelling, pushing and struggling. The American bombers had taken out the bridge, and people jammed to the bridge entrance. Poor people. Hundreds of them swarmed the broken, shapeless bridge, some of them scaling the buckled steel truss at the topside and some below. What remained of the bridge were the twisted steel beams and the angle irons which hung in the air helplessly in all directions, and yet people clawed and crawled their way for hours to the other side. Many of them fell off the junk pile of a bridge and plunged to death below into the icy river. The war did strange things to people. Some braved the bitter cold water by hanging on to the half-drowned bridge section and waded across to the other side. The river water was already forming icy slush in late November, foretelling the bitterly cold winter yet to come. Surveying the situation, we didn't like any of the options we faced. Americans had a pontoon bridge installed, but only the American soldiers were allowed to cross it. Civilians were not permitted to go on it.

Swimming across the river was out of question, so we decided to get away from the pandemonium. We fought our way out of the desperate crowds and walked downstream away from Pyongyang toward west. I knew of a town called Taepyong, near the mouth of the Daedong River, where I used to teach. I figured that I would find someone I knew there. We walked for a day or so and we reached the mouth of the river, where we saw a tiny boat ferrying people across the river. We piled into the tiny boat with the other desperate refugees and crossed the river. Haeju was the main destination straight down south through Hwanghae Province. All the refugees were headed for Haeju, and we joined them. We would have had an easier time on the main highway to Haeju, but it was open for military use exclusively, the retreating U.N. and the Southern troops, and closed to the public.

We took the back roads to Haeju, which took us longer than we liked, but it turned out to be for the best. I don't recall how many days we walked, but when we reached the outskirts of Haeju the sun was setting, and we decided to stay in a small village for the night.

We met an old man there who told us, "If you want to travel south you must go toward Yonan. If you go to Haeju, you'll run into difficulties."

In time of war your purpose in life is clear and simple: staying alive. All of your senses are tuned to matters of living and dying. Sight, sound, smell, touch, and taste are your allies. You trust your senses and the instincts that rise from them. I was faced with a decision, whether to go to Haeju or Yonan. I had no information about either place. It's like that in time of war. You have very little information on anything. You don't have time to check on the reliability of the information when a stranger tells you something.

I looked at the wrinkled old man who was smoking a long skinny pipe made out of bamboo. He didn't appear to be affected by the war one way or the other. The way he drew on the pipe so calmly, he could have been enjoying an after-dinner smoke following a birthday celebration for his grandson. I resisted my urge to ask him why he suggested Yonan in lieu of Haeju. I wanted to ask him a lot of questions, but his demeanor was such that he couldn't care less whether or not I took his advice and that he had already said all he was going to say about it. His half-closed eyes were kind and wise, and his white beard was well groomed. I decided that he had no reason to deceive me or lead me astray. Whatever you think and do in time of war, you know that every little thing matters greatly, and I decided to trust him. My fellow refugees from Chestnut Grove, Mr. Lee and Mr. Park, and I discussed the merits of going to Yonan like the old man said. "But everyone is going to Haeju," they said.

"Yes, I know, but…"

In the morning we headed for Yonan, which turned out to be the correct choice. All the Haeju refugees were caught and returned to Pyongyang later.

At Yonan we piled into another small boat like sardines

and headed for Inchon. Luckily we were in the middle of the pack. The boat rode dangerously low, and when the water splashed over the deck, the people on the outside were pushed off.

Inchon was the port city on which General MacArthur had led the brilliant surprise landing three months earlier, cutting off the supply line to the North Korean army that concentrated around the Busan perimeter. Busan perimeter was the final stand for the U.N. and the Southern armies. With their backs against the ocean 70 miles away in the southeastern corner of the peninsula, they were in danger of being swept into the ocean.

This was happening about the time when my father was organizing underground meetings in Chestnut Grove. The communists were claiming a total victory day after day in the name of the people and the fatherland. But father stayed with his belief that the Soviets and the communist north would perish eventually. He just kept saying, "The Soviets are bad." Perhaps he saw the fundamental flaw in the Soviet system and what it did to the Korean people. When he repeated, "The Soviets are bad," maybe he was referring to the miles and miles of trucks that lined the road from Korea to the Soviet border. Those Soviet trucks (GMC trucks from the lend-lease program during World War Ⅱ) were loaded with Korean goods. Or, maybe he was referring to the indiscriminate raping spree the Soviet soldiers engaged in and their general disregard for humanity.

Whatever the vision my father had regarding the demise of the communists, the reality was that the democratic forces behind the Busan perimeter was about to collapse. He didn't know, nor did I, that the American generals and the policy makers in Washington were debating the fate of the peninsula, whether or not the tiny peninsula called Korea was worth defending with American lives. The American public was dubious, their opinions were divided. Some pointed to the Secretary of State Dean Acheson's statement of January 1950: that Korea was not a part of American defense perimeter. It was MacArthur who convinced Washington that the defense against communism in Asia was crucial in the defensive effort against communism in Europe, and the Joint Chiefs of Staff approved MacArthur's plan to double back around to Inchon. The Inchon landing by the American X Corps and the 1st Marine Division was dubbed a military miracle. They advanced to Seoul and recaptured the capital on September 28th. Caught in a crossfire, the communist forces faltered and retreated back to the North. The U.N.

and the South Korean armies pursued the defeated Northern army. The Eighth Army led by General Walker captured Pyongyang, while the South Korean troops entered Wonsan on the east coast. Together, they continued the pursuit to the Yalu River bordering China while MacArthur demanded surrender to Premier Kim Il Sung.

My father was ecstatic that the democratic forces were on the move to rid of communism, even though Kim Il Sung refused to surrender on the radio on October 10th. My father exclaimed, "This is the end of communism in the fatherland!" Tae Geuk flags flew high again. He had done his part rooting out the communists in Chestnut Grove in concert with the global struggle between democracy and communism, not knowing that the tide would soon turn again.

About 100 miles to the north of Chestnut Grove, 300,000 Chinese communist soldiers lay waiting in the snow, ready to ambush the advancing U.N. forces. They had begun infiltrating into the peninsula about the same time the Eighth Army entered Pyongyang, and the American intelligence grossly underestimated the concentration of the Chinese troops. In his public address, Chou En Lai warned the Chinese intervention, its intention to help the North Korean forces, but MacArthur didn't consider the warning seriously.

"They appeared out of nowhere," as many veterans said later. Outfitted in white parkas, the Chinese employed the "human wave" tactic in countering the U.N. pursuit. Although they were ill equipped, the Chinese rushed the American positions in great numbers and literally over-ran them. Surprised by the sheer numbers, the U.N. forces pulled back south, allowing the communist forces to enter Chestnut Grove, Pyongyang and now Haeju. Had my father known about the magnitude of the counter assault and its global significance, would he have decided to guard Chestnut Grove with measly band of forty untrained men and the few rounds of ammunition?

I wonder about that sometimes.

He would have been better off packing up his family and escaping the certain death with the rest of the villagers.

Would I have thought otherwise about returning to Chestnut Grove within a week? If I had known then what I know now, would I have taken my mother, brother, and the little ones with me?

Yes.

By the time I landed in Inchon, there was no trace of General MacArthur, General Almond, the X Corps, and the

1st Marine Division. The city was functioning as a town, with a few buildings knocked out here and there along with several destroyed Soviet made tanks. The reason I went to Inchon was because of a relative by the name of Oh Byung-lin, supposedly the Chief of Police in Inchon. At the mention of Uncle Oh's name, the policemen in Inchon were happy to see us. As it turned out Uncle Oh was not the Chief but an assistant Chief and he had just transferred to another city called Echun. I asked them where it was, and they drove us to Echun. That was the end of December 1950, and I had been on the run for over a month.

I didn't get too much rest in Echun, either. Just as we arrived there the massive retreat of January 4th began, and I was on the run again along with the retreating U.N. forces. Seoul was in danger of falling again to the communist troops, and I walked to Suwon and caught a train south. I found a space on the roof of a train, pressing my hands, my buttocks and my feet flat against the rounded rooftop lest I slide off as the train rocked, started and stopped. Still, I was happy to find my space on the roof of the train. Down below, a mob of people wailed and cried for want of a space like mine, and people ran and chased the train as it pulled out of Suwon station. I rode it for a little while. I didn't even get to Daejon before I was kicked off the train, and I walked the rest of the way to Daejon, Kyungju, and on to Busan, a long mountainous walk of about 300 miles all together.

In Busan, I didn't know anyone, had no place to go. In today's terms, I was homeless, a street person. I wandered about the city, looking for food and a place to camp for the night. Mostly I starved, and I ate when someone offered leftovers. Someone suggested that I go down to the harbor and see if they were hiring workers, and I went down there. I saw a lot of refugees like me hauling boxes on and off the American military cargo ship. Luckily, I was hired. I was weak but I worked hard, knowing that there would be food later. Some of the workers couldn't wait to eat. Once in a while they broke out the C-ration boxes and opened the cans and gulped them down when no one was looking. During the day a co-worker opened a box and handed out the cans for us to take out of the port at the end of the day. Everyone tucked the can under their shirts, and so did I. At the end of the day all of the co-workers exited the gate safely. I was caught. Probably because I was skinny and the bulk of the can was too obvious. Or, perhaps my petrified face out of fear of getting caught. I was caught nevertheless, and my first encounter with an American turned out to be an ordeal I'll never forget.

The guard hauled me to a place called the "MP STATION," where a huge military policeman was stoking a fire in a potbelly stove. The policeman gave me a piercing look, and I shuddered. In the meantime he jabbed at the hot coal with the red hot metal poker. I had heard that the American soldiers branded your forehead with "Thief" if they caught you stealing and I thought that the policeman was intending to do exactly that. It is amazing what you believe in time of war, especially when you are hungry. I believed that the big man was going to brand my forehead and I put my hands together and rubbed them together like I was praying to the gods. He was yelling in his booming voice, and I had no idea what he was saying. Whatever he was yelling about, I prayed and bowed, asking him to give me a break this one time, and he had no idea what I was saying. I pleaded in Korean over and over, and he stopped yelling finally.

Then he stood up suddenly and grabbed my collar and pounded on my chest once, twice, and he dragged me to the door and pushed me out of the door, yelling, "Get out!" I didn't know what that meant at the time, but as soon as he released me I ran like the dickens and got out of there fast.

I couldn't work at the harbor any more after the incident and I looked for other work. I must have had what they called the "people fortune." While I was making inquiries about work, I ran across someone from Chestnut Grove, who told me that he had seen my Uncle Je-yong, my father's younger brother from Pyongyang. He was the very policeman uncle I was supposed to flee with from Pyongyang. He had been seen in Kwangbok Dong, and I dashed down there and began looking for him everywhere for a whole day. I finally saw him at a vending stand where he was working as a cloth cutter. We were both happy to see each other. We didn't know what to say to each other and felt as though we were seeing ghosts. I was happy and surprised to see him alive and he was happy to see me alive. It was like that in wartime.

Uncle Je-yong was speechless, trying to hold back tears, though not too well, and after a while he gave me some money.

"First, go take a bath," he said.

chapter 4

CHESTNUT VENDOR

The bath was heavenly. In a public bathhouse with a large hot tub as big as a swimming pool, I shed the grungy clothes that had been stuck to me for two months and slid myself into the steaming hot water. I wondered where and how they had acquired the precious water. So much water. Early every morning I'd wake up to the sounds of vicious quarreling coming from the neighborhood well. Women lined up behind the water well at the crack of the dawn and they jostled and argued for their turn at the water for cooking breakfast.

I couldn't remember the last time I had a bath as I scrubbed the dirt from the war, the sweat on top of sweat from running through the hills in Chestnut Grove, the rubble of Pyongyang, the boat ride across Daedong River, the long walk south through Hwanghae Province, the ride on the rickety boat to Inchon, then Echun, the walk to Suwon and the train ride on top of the train, and the soot from the exhaust through Kyunggi Province, then the 300 mile walk to Busan.

As I stayed submerged in the hot tub, I felt the layers of dirt melt away along with the sharp edge that came with the war and the hunger. None of my journey made sense. I felt numb to the fact that I had lost my cousin, my father, my uncle and maybe my brothers, my mother and my sisters.

I closed my eyes and tried to remember the good things from my childhood in Chestnut Grove and my teaching days. I had been a respected teacher in Pyongyang, and in Busan I was in the MP station by the harbor scared out of my wits, afraid that an American soldier was going to brand my forehead.

Maybe my luck was changing. I found Uncle Je-yong, didn't I? And here I was taking a bath, something that had not even occurred to me for months. What a sight I must have been to him.

After the bath Uncle Je-yong bought me new clothes and helped me find a boarding house. I didn't have to look for a place to camp out for a day. I was no longer homeless. I began thinking about what to do for a living, and I saw a chestnut vendor. Roasted chestnuts! Roasting chestnuts was something I knew about. Chestnut Grove was my hometown, for heaven's sake, and I'd been roasting chestnuts ever since I was a tiny kid.

Uncle Je-yong helped me set up a vending stand at an intersection in Kwangbok Dong. Normally a chestnut roasting stand had a squatty, round, hibachi type stove that burned wood charcoal with a metal grill. But my stand was no ordinary roasting stand. I bought a large used cast iron wok from a metal dealer and I cleaned it shiny and black. I built a wood charcoal stove to fit the round bottom of the wok so that the stove could heat the wok evenly. Then I got hold of pebble rocks and washed them clean. I dumped the pebble rocks in the wok, then a sack of chestnuts, and sprayed a handful of sugar on the chestnuts as they cooked. The pebbles turned black and shiny from the sugar resin and the chestnuts turned light brown and gold as I stirred the whole lot with a wooden oar-like spoon. That's how you make the Pyongyang style roasted chestnuts, and I put on a show as the wok produced the sweet smelling aroma that turned everyone's head.

I sold chestnuts like a mad man. I hawked the chestnuts

shamelessly, yelling at the passers-by, "Straight from Pyongyang, I have chestnuts from Pyongyang!"

People stopped and asked me how I could get chestnuts from Pyongyang. There was a war going on.

I just smiled and kept on yelling, "Pyongyang chestnuts here," and people bought my roasted chestnuts by the bags, and on a good day, I sold more than a bushel of chestnuts.

Uncle Je-yong and the people around were shocked to see how well the business was doing. I just smiled and said, "Maybe business is my fate."

I continued on with the chestnut vending for a year and I managed to pay my rent at the boarding house and eat square meals and have some money left over. My life was taking shape in a routine of sorts, and I began thinking about what to do with my life. It was 1952, the 22nd year of my life, and I thought I should do more than chestnut vending. I decided that I should go to a university if I was going to get anywhere in a new town in a new society called South Korea. Looking back, my decision to continue my schooling was an important turning point in my life.

If I was going to attend a university, I thought I should go for a well known school like Seoul National, Yonhee(Yonsei) or Korea University. I checked into all three of the schools and I found out that Seoul National University didn't have a branch campus, and Korea University had a branch campus in Taegu, a city about 100 miles away.

Yonsei University had just established a satellite campus in Busan, and one of the professors at Yonsei happened to be from Chestnut Grove. The professor suggested that I apply to Yonsei, and I filed an application with Yonsei and its physics department in February that year.

I took the entrance examination and I passed it. A problem arose with the application, though. At 22, I was at an age for the military service, and the university policy required that I fulfil the military service in order to enroll.

In wartime, military service came first before anything else, and I applied for the Army Officers Training School. I might as well become an officer, I thought, as long as I was going to join the army. I passed all the written tests. But I didn't pass the physical. I was small and skinny to begin with. Moreover, the life of a refugee had taken a toll on my body, and I weighed in at 95 pounds. The Officers Training School turned me down, as I did not meet the minimum weight requirement for the service. Let me tell you, I was not unhappy that I flunked the examination. All of my friends who went to the Officers School and became officers died in battles. I considered myself lucky even though I felt bad for my friends who died on the frontline.

I enrolled in the physics department at Yonsei University with the money I earned from chestnut roasting. It was difficult to give up the hard-earned money, but education was the best investment I could make. A student by day and a chestnut vendor by night, I had a new purpose in life, and I was as happy as a young refugee could be away from home.

Meanwhile, the combined North Korean and Chinese forces of 486,000 armed with Soviet equipment pushed the action further south near the 38th parallel, and my hope of returning home waned as days went by. The city of Busan was inundated with refugees like me, millions from northern provinces, whose fate hung on the 365,000 U.N. and South Korean troops.

The refugees from northern provinces were considered an odd lot. Even though we subscribed to the principles of democracy, no one appreciated it. As far as the locals were concerned in Busan and in the surrounding region, we were perceived as intruders in their otherwise peaceful home. We took away their jobs, they said, and our presence exacerbated the food shortage problem.

"You refugees eat so much," they sneered.

When the outhouse tanks filled up, they clamored, "You refugees shit so much." And so on.

You get the picture.

More often, the locals looked at us with disdain rather than with compassion. And yet, if the communists kept on advancing and reached Busan, the refugees would be the first ones to face the firing squad because of the "traitorous act" we committed against the fatherland.

No compassion there, either.

We gathered in front of the newspaper that was posted on the board every morning and we talked anxiously about the advancing communist army. The details were sketchy at best, in the newspapers or radio, and we relied on the newly arriving refugees for information.

The fall of Seoul was a devastating blow, and we felt as though the end was near. My father was wrong: communists were not going away. But we cheered when the allies recaptured the capital as though our lives had been saved. Then we could hope again. We hoped that the Allies would push back so that we could all go home.

Little did we know that, about this time, Washington was talking anxiously about evacuating the troops to Japan, faced with the seriousness of the Chinese intervention. They were also considering a retreat to Cheju Island, about 100 miles off the southern coast. Thank goodness that didn't happen.

We heard a rumor then that MacArthur was going to make a move against Red China much like the Inchon operation. That didn't happen either. Next thing we heard was that MacArthur was relieved of his command, and we wondered what was going to happen.

Rumors flew about. The wartime rumors.

The Soviet army was ready to enter the war. Formosa troops were coming. Atom bomb was coming. There were a lot of rumors about the atom bomb.

As it turned out, the war came to a standstill around the 38th parallel. Both sides took turns in all-out assault operations with little success. Coupled with the tremendous pressure from the world community for a negotiated settlement rather than escalating the scope of the war, truce talks began in late 1951. It took them one year and nine months and numerous skirmishes in between before they came to terms and signed the armistice agreement in July, 1953.

The armistice agreement called for a DMZ(Demilitarized Zone), a strip of land two and a half miles wide and 150 miles long across the waist of the peninsula through the fields and mountains from its west coast to the east. Although the truce was signed, the DMZ was now a mine-field fortified with two million troops at both sides of the zone, and there was no chance in hell that I could go home.

chapter 5

HUNG SA DAHN

Home was where I made it.

The truce brought Yonsei University back to Seoul, and I followed. Seoul was my home now, and I felt less like a refugee there. In Seoul, my life began as a university student, not as a homeless wanderer in sore need of a bath.

However, I had a tougher time in Seoul, financially. Chestnut vending was a roaring success in Busan, but in Seoul, the mere mention of Pyongyang drew ire from the pedestrians, my potential customers. Selling chestnuts from Pyongyang was out of the question, or even the Pyongyang "style" chestnuts. There was another problem. The police were on the lookout for any and every young men in my age to check on their military service status, and if you didn't have the right papers, they hauled you in immediately. I didn't have the paper that exempted me from the military service, and with my Pyongyang accent, they would have suspected me of being a communist spy for sure. So the chestnut vending was not an option for me. My only option was to stay in school uniform to avoid the hassle and the possible torture.

But then I needed to make money in order to remain in school. Talk about a vicious circle, I found myself worrying about where to sleep day after day, and tuition became a big problem. Even bus fare was a problem. I didn't devote much time to my studies, since the most of my time went to making ends meet. The head of the physics department, Professor Chang Gi-won, didn't have any sympathy for my situation. He scolded me mercilessly for my poor performance in school.

How well I remember that day. He didn't understand, nor did I tell him that I spent my days selling used military clothes and the goods from an American military base to an acquaintance in Yongwol, Kangwon Province, about 120 miles southeast of Seoul. But Professor Chang was only interested in my academic devotion, such as it was, and I avoided him like a plague whenever I was on campus.

My life improved though, thanks to the trading business in

Yongwol, and Uncle Je-yong's help. I was free to move about with the borrowed identification card from my uncle, which said that I was a detective. Whenever the police stopped me on streets and trains, I produced the identification card, and the officers left me alone, thank goodness.

I began tutoring as well, and I was able to come up with the tuition for the first semester and enough money to live on. For the second semester, however, I didn't have enough money and I couldn't enroll in school. When I wasn't working, I went to school and hung around the campus for a while and came home.

It was during this time that Mr. Lee Kwan-sung asked me to join Hung Sa Dahn. My father had told me about Hung Sa Dahn, so I was familiar with the organization that Dosan Ahn Chang-Ho had founded back in 1913. Mr. Lee Kwan-sung and my father were old friends from Chestnut Grove, and I had sought his advice on occasion.

I started to frequent the Hung Sa Dahn office and I found it far more comforting than wandering about the campus and watching my friends and others walk to classes for study. I also ran into Mr. Choi Hee-song, an original Hung Sa Dahn member who had worked with Dosan himself. Mr. Choi was from Pyongyang and he looked after me as his own.

I felt as though I had found a home away from home. Kindness and consideration were not commonplace, but rare qualities in people in the aftermath of a war. Hung Sa Dahn folks were far different from the usual Seoulites, who were known for being cold-hearted, crafty and cunning. As the saying went, "Keep your eyes on your nose. Seoul people will steal your nose from you," but the Hung Sa Dahn people were the opposite and they were genuinely interested in my well-being.

One of the best things that happened to me at Hung Sa Dahn was my meeting with Madame Ahn Hyung-saeng. She was the first daughter of Patriot Ahn Jung Geun. Because she was a daughter of the man who was revered by all Koreans as a leader in the independence movement against Imperial Japan during the earlier part of the 20th century, she was a busy lady.

When I met her for the first time she reminded me of my mother. I hovered around her, and she regarded me as a helpful young man. I offered my help whenever I could, and she appreciated it. Soon, I was making telephone calls for her and going to the post office for her. She needed an assistant or a secretary to help her with scheduling and coordinating her meetings and interviews, and I became her de-facto assistant and secretary.

In those days there was no private telephone, and I didn't know of anyone who owned a telephone. The only telephone I saw was at the Hung Sa Dahn office, and it was not a good one, either.

So I walked everywhere to see the people I needed to see in arranging interviews for her, and the time and places for the commemoration services for her father and other patriots in the independence movement. Many times, the people I needed to see weren't in their offices, and I waited for them for hours. Sometimes I returned the next day and so forth. Whatever the task, I followed through until it was completed, and Madame Ahn, now advanced in age, appreciated all my legwork.

She needed help around the house as well, and I did the chores as a son would for his mother. I am proud to say that she was pleased to have me around. I was practically an orphan, and she treated me like the son she never had.

At meetings with people like General Lee Bom-suk, her closest friend, and former Vice President Yi Shi-young and Mr. Hahm Tae-young, an independence fighter, she would introduce me to them without fail. In return I helped her friends as much as I could, which exposed me to the world I never knew before. Working for them provided me with the opportunity to have broader views and the impetus for big dreams.

Another unforgettable figure in my life is Chu Yo-han *sunsaeng*. He was a brilliant poet and a writer from Pyongyang, and he was very pleased to hear that I had taught at the First Middle School of Pyongyang. A student at the Second Middle School of Pyongyang, Chu *sunsaeng* shared his young days in Pyongyang with me. Later in 1954 he ran for a seat in the National Assembly against Mr. Yoon Po-sun in Chongno District, and I helped Chu *sunsaeng* with the electoral campaign. He was also a founding member of Hung Sa Dahn and he played an important role in my journey to America.

I don't remember exactly when or how, but the idea of going to America came to me like beating drums. I was drawn to the idea to the point of obsession and I couldn't sleep at night. Considering the fact that only the sons and the daughters of the rich and the powerful were able to go to America to study in those days, my idea was impractical, to say the least. Nevertheless, the thought persisted like a calling from somewhere far away and I never stopped thinking about it. It was my destiny, I had decided, even before I knew anything about America, the language, the culture, and the people.

My only contact with the Americans was in the MP station in Busan. My experience there was not an inspiring one, especially because I was convinced that the big guy was going to brand my forehead with a white-hot metal poker. And yet, the encounter did not influence my view of America.

To me, America represented strength and goodness, as evidenced by the food, the clothes and the mighty tanks. They brought their food–meat, vegetables and sundries–in metal cans from thousands of miles away, and I was fascinated with the technology and the wealth the canned food represented. The clothes were made strong and durable with the heavy-duty material, wonderful stitches, and the good workmanship.

I told my friends, classmates and the folks at Hung Sa Dahn that I was going to America. They were surprised and dubious at my resolution, probably wondering whether I was drunken or sober. They knew that I didn't drink or smoke at all, so they thought there was something else that steered my sights towards America. After the first shock, some of my friends said, "Good thinking," or "Wonderful," while the majority of the people said, "What?" All of them thought that it was impossible for me to even think about going to America, a person like me who had neither money, nor family to support me.

I pushed on, nevertheless, and the new goal took me away from the loneliness I felt, especially on holidays when everyone was busy with their families. I suppose I could have gone to my friends', but it was difficult for me to join them, and I was afraid of spoiling the holiday mood of the others.

Living without a family was a reminder of the war and the countless tragic stories that unfolded afterwards. Those who didn't know my background invariably asked me about my family, and I had to talk about my escape from the North, my father's execution, my younger brother who wanted to come with me, and my mother, who had no way of knowing whether I was alive or dead. It was not easy for a young man of twenty-four to explain these things, how he had managed to come to the South alone.

Except my friends and a few kind people I knew from Hung Sa Dahn, people in general regarded me as a nuisance like an unwelcome guest with a disease. I had never thought

I would be treated like this in the land famous for its hospitality.

Mother had always fed guests first, even though the guests came unannounced. People used to drop in and stay as long as they wished and that's how visitors were treated before the war.

A traveler would come to the door after nightfall and ask, "I am traveling through the village. Could you put me up for the night?"

"Sure. Please come in."

Mother would bring up a food tray to the guestroom, and I would follow into the room. Mother would set down the food tray and leave. I would stay behind and listen to the conversation between father and the traveler, fascinated to hear about the faraway places like Seoul, the streetcars, the tall buildings, and the huge department stores.

I knew then that I would go to a big place like Seoul someday to study and to live. I was in Seoul at last, but Seoul was not at all like the place I imagined as a boy. Under normal circumstances, I would go back home to mother, my brother and my sisters, but the road seemed to be shut forever as the political situation between the south and the north worsened.

Did the war make our hearts cold and apathetic? I asked this question often. It was easy to blame everything on the war: corrupt politicians, poverty, thousands of beggars, orphans, and limb-less war veterans that roamed the streets of Seoul. Yet, rich people possessed their own cars and lived in houses with tall cement fences topped with barbed wire and jagged pieces of glasses from liquor bottles.

Nobody opened the door to a weary traveler in want of food and sleep. The angel in my mother and the same angel in the old man with the white beard who fed me and guided me away from Haeju were but a distant memory from a different world.

It seemed that the war came as an agent of death and destruction, followed by another explosion—cruel hearts. It was time for me to move on.

Once I set my mind to my journey to America, I ran across many more Hung Sa Dahn people who had studied and lived in America. When they heard about my plans, they told me about others who were already in America and those who were getting ready to go there. I gained more confidence about my decision as time went on and I made inquiries into the overseas study program. I collected all the forms that I needed to fill out, and there were a lot of them as my friends had warned me. I didn't know where to begin but I figured that I needed to get into a school first. I went to the American library and found a couple of application forms for the University of Oregon.

Why Oregon, I didn't know, but it was one of the forms I picked up, filled out, and sent. There were others, but I can't remember which schools they were. Besides, I couldn't afford to send too many applications, for the postage to America added up quickly. Some of them required an application fee, and I dropped them off my list immediately.

When the reply came from the University of Oregon some months later, I was flabbergasted to find a letter of admission in the envelope. I was happy of course, but I didn't know what it meant in terms of the process. What now? I asked everyone I could.

The tests came next. I studied and took the tests at the Ministry of Education to qualify for the foreign studies. I passed the tests at my first attempt. Then came the English test at the American Embassy. I studied the old tests that my friends gave me at school, and I memorized them line by line not knowing what any of them meant. I was nervous about my English proficiency, but I managed to pass the test, though just barely.

Then came the real hurdle. The money. I needed a sponsor who would take on the financial responsibility for my schooling in America, and I didn't know anyone who could. My uncle was ecstatic that I passed the tests and qualified for the study-abroad, but he was in no position to aid me financially, not on a policeman's salary. Then I realized why only rich kids, or sons and daughters of congressmen were able to go to America to study. I was only day dreaming about going to America, after all.

I nearly gave up the idea until I saw Mr. Chu Yo-han one day at the Hung Sa Dahn office. He asked me when I was going to America, and I told him, "I passed all the tests, but I can't go because I don't have a financial sponsor."

He looked at me thoughtfully and said, "I'll try to find you one."

Speechless, I stared at him for a long time as though an angel appeared in front of me. All I could say was, "Pardon me?"

Mr. Chu nodded and repeated, "I'll try to find someone for you."

With that, he lifted me out of the depressed state I was in, and for the first time in my life, I began to pray. Two weeks went by, but Mr. Chu wasn't very hopeful. This was the end of the road for sure. If Mr. Chu couldn't do it, it wasn't going to happen at all, simple as that.

Then he came up with an idea that changed the course of my life. He said, "There's one more place I can try. Hung Sa Dahn in America sponsors Korean students, and I'll write to Mr. Song Jong-ik about you."

Mr. Song was a well-known figure around Hung Sa Dahn. He was one of the founding members of the organization when Dosan Ahn Chang-Ho founded it in San Francisco in 1913. Hung Sa Dahn was born in America 17 years before I was born in Chestnut Grove, and it continues to exist today, seventy-one years later.

Looking back, I did not fully appreciate what Hung Sa Dahn was about then. At age twenty-five, I had only a vague notion of what it was even though I had prepared for the exhaustive admission process of Hung Sa Dahn. The admission process ended with a 4-hour oral examination in front of four or five elder members. That was the most grueling examination I had ever gone through.

The interview board fired questions at me like a machine gun:

Who are you?

Why are you in school?

What do you study?

Why do you study?

Why do you want to be a better person?

What do you mean by becoming a better person?

Who is Dosan *sunsaeng*?

What are his teachings?

Why did he teach us to tell truth always?

What did he mean by "To love oneself is to love others?"

What does "The love of country" mean to you?

What is Hung Sa Dahn?

Why did Dosan *sunsaeng* form Hung Sa Dahn?

Why did he see the need to train the young people?

What was the independence movement?

What was the essence of his conversation with Ito Hirobumi?

The questions never stopped, and I floundered many times. It was evident to the questioners and to myself that I was not prepared for the test. Instead of producing good answers, I produced a lot of sweat down my back, and I was certain that I failed the interrogatory. Had I known that the entire questioning was based on the Socratic method, I would have been more relaxed. Instead I likened the process to torture, and it took a lot out of me, and left me with a huge headache.

To my surprise, Mr. Park Hyun-hwan came to my rescue, saying, "Mr. Paik, according to the strict rules, your performance today was a failure. But considering that you are a busy student, we will admit you along with the other applicants. I know you will study and learn more about Hung Sa Dahn as you go."

I lowered my head and kept quiet, for I knew I had gotten away with mediocrity. It made me think about my life in general, though, and I thanked the Lord that I found a home.

Hung Sa Dahn made me feel like a whole person: I was simply Korean, not a refugee from the north.

The angel was alive and well, soon to rescue me yet once again.

chapter 6

FOREIGNER

Mr. Chu Yo-han was smiling effusively, and I knew he had good news.

"The American Hung Sa Dahn is planning to sponsor two students annually, along with a $500 scholarship for each. They want you to come to America," he said.

This was far more than I ever expected. The sponsorship was considered more difficult than snatching a star out of the sky, and here I was, hearing but not yet believing that I had a sponsor, Mr. Song Jong-ik. He had no way of knowing who I was and what I was like other than what Mr. Chu had described, "a fine young Hung Sa Dahn member." Just like that, Mr. Song and the American Hung Sa Dahn were willing to take on the responsibility for me.

I had an angel after all.

America was a reality now, and when I came to my senses, I saw Mr. Chu smiling at me. I stammered, "Thank you,"
about a thousand times and I think I bowed to him as many
times.

It took another year to pull together the rest of the items:
the passport, the visa, airfare, and traveling money. When I
picked up the passport from the Foreign Office, I held,

rubbed, smelled, and flipped through it over and over. It was hard to believe that I had a passport in my hand, three years after I set my mind on America.

As for the airplane ticket, my uncle gave me some money. Together with the money I had saved, I exchanged them at the government bank for one hundred U.S. dollars. In those days, the government allowed the overseas bound students to exchange up to five hundred U.S. dollars. I took my $100 to the black market, where the U.S. dollar was worth more than the rate set by the government, and sold them for twice the original amount. Then I went back to the government bank and exchanged the money for $200. That's how I bought the airplane ticket.

I bought a couple of shirts and new shoes. Someone had said that I could make a lot of money with *kim* in Japan during the overnight stopover on the way to America, and I jumped on the idea. With whatever money I had left over I bought *kim*, the paper-thin black seaweed for wrapping sushi rolls. Korean *kim* was considered the best by the Japanese people. I filled my trunk with it. But when I arrived at Haneda airport in Japan, the customs officers checked through the trunk filled with the packets of *kim*. They smiled politely and said that I could take in only ten packets into town, and leave the remainder in the transit warehouse and claim them on my way out to America. I offered to pay the customs duty for the *kim*, but they shook their heads and said that there was no trade agreement between Korea and Japan, and that there was nothing they could do. I checked in the *kim* packets at the transit warehouse and I stuffed the ten *kim* packets into my small overnight bag.

The bus ride into Tokyo was grim. The *kim* was supposed to put about $500 in my pocket, the seed money to start off my life in America, but no such luck for me.

I looked out the window and stared into the stream of lights on lamp posts and windows, the same lights that I had seen from the air. The sea of night-lights fascinated me, for no night-lights were in Korea on account of the war and the shortage of electricity for many years afterwards.

Next morning I took out the ten *kim* packets and walked across the street from the hotel. I sold the *kim* in the matter of minutes. If the customs hadn't intercepted the trunk load, I would have made $500 easily. But I made only $50, which was better than nothing. Those stinking customs people, I said to myself and got ready for the PanAm airplane that was waiting to take me to Honolulu. Collecting my trunk filled with *kim*, I boarded the DC-4, the twin propeller clipper, along with twenty or so other passengers.

The airplane raced down the runway, and my anticipation soared. On my way to America! Across the Pacific Ocean! The ocean stretched forever. At first I was fascinated with the endless body of water and the clouds below. Then the monotony took its toll on me, and I dozed off. I woke up now and then just to make sure that the endless sky and the sea were still there. Then I dozed off.

Descending down the ramp stairs onto the tarmac in Honolulu was an event I'll never forget. As soon as I stepped out of the airplane, the fragrance of the Hawaiian flowers hit me like a gust of hot wind. I forgot all about the long, boring, airplane ride. As I stepped off the boarding ramp holding the winter coat in my arm, a pretty girl dressed in grass skirt came up to me and draped a lei over my head with a smile and an "aloha." Not sure what to think of the ritual, I bowed sheepishly and followed the other passengers to the terminal and then on to the cafeteria.

The passengers sat down at the tables here and there, and I sat down, too. A waitress came and said something. Without saying a word I produced a lunch coupon that came with the airplane ticket. She said something else (most likely she asked me what I wanted to eat), and I smiled and nodded. A while later she brought me a hamburger and French fries.

Mind you, I had never seen a hamburger in my life. I stooped over and examined the round thing, which appeared to be two thick round pieces of bread holding a round piece of meat and some greens. It smelled good and it made my mouth water, but I had no idea how to go about eating it. The waitress didn't give me any chopsticks, just a knife and a metal contraption that looked like a comb with a handle. The hamburger was too big for chopsticks anyway, I thought, and I continued to look at it with more curiosity than appetite.

Then I heard a familiar language bark out at me. A Korean voice from a passer-by.

The stranger said, "Just pick it up with your hand and bite on it. That's how you eat the hamburger!"

I turned around and looked at the older man dressed in a uniform, holding a broom and a dustpan. Surprised and happy to hear the Korean speaking, I turned to him and yelled out, "*Ajocee!*" But before I could say anything else, he kept on walking, having said all he wanted to. I had so much to ask him.

With the old man gone, I focused on the hamburger again. Remembering what he said, I picked it up with my two hands, even though I felt like a barbarian doing it. I took a healthy bite, and the meat juice splattered in my mouth like honey. I forgot all about the awkwardness of grabbing foodstuff by hand then. I finished my first hamburger ever, my hands dripping with the juices and the bits of tomato seeds. Oh, and the tasty French fries... I could eat them all day.

After the meal I went to the bathroom and washed my hands. Figuring that it was time for me to use the commode, I pushed the door open to a toilet to find an oblong ceramic bowl with water in it. It was not a commode I was accustomed to. Giving it a glance, I didn't dare to use it, for I was not prepared to meet yet another challenge in the new world.

I should have done a better job in my preparation for the journey, I told myself. I should have known about the hamburger, which seemed like the most common food around. I should have known about the western style toilet. But then how could I have known? Out of all the people who had been to America, no one told me about these important things, and I wondered if they had ever really been in

America. I walked around a while, keeping my eyes on the other passengers from my flight. We boarded the airplane again for the 9-hour ride to Los Angeles.

Los Angeles was not as warm as Honolulu, yet I was boiling under the layers of winter clothing. It was January 7th, after all, in the middle of the winter, and it made sense to bundle up. Not so in Los Angeles. I wanted to take off the sweaters and the heavy undershirt badly and walk around in short sleeves like everyone else. But I had no place to put them in; my trunk was filled with *kim* and a heavy overcoat. So I just kept the layers of sweaters on me, sweating like a pig.

Nevertheless, I was happy and excited in anticipation of meeting the Hung Sa Dahn people and I gave the girl at the Pan Am telephone counter the Hung Sa Dahn number which I had committed to my memory, REpublic 2320. She smiled and dialed the number and talked into the telephone while I watched her anxiously. She handed the telephone and smiled again, gesturing for me to talk on the telephone. Mr. Ha Hee-ok was at the other end, and I have never been so happy to hear a Korean voice.

He had bad news for me though: Mr. Song Jong-ik had passed away the day before. I could not believe it. When Mr. Ha came to the airport to pick me up, I asked him if it was really true. He nodded quietly and he drove me to the funeral home where Mr. Song lay resting. I felt as though it was my fault that he died of a brain hemorrhage at the age of sixty-nine, and I became apprehensive about my new start in America. After the service Mr. Ha took me to the Hung Sa Dahn office, a house on Catalina Avenue with several rooms for students like me. It was my home for the time being.

I didn't sleep at all that night. On the strange bed in the strange land I tossed and turned, unable to find a comfortable spot. *Did I do the right thing by coming to America? What would father say? What would mother say? Is she alive? My poor brother. I wonder how he is. And my little sisters. Will I ever go home?*

Images of Chestnut Grove played throughout the night like scenes from a silent movie: anxious father coming down the hill with a rifle in his hands, mother and younger sisters smiling, my older sister's worried face, my uncle's face back in Seoul, and Young-ik, my little brother, who ran up the hill in his bare feet to catch up with me that early morning.

Strangely, his image had a voice: "*Hyung*, my big brother, I'm here." He wanted to come with me wherever I was going. He wanted to run away with me from the crackling sounds of guns all around the valley. But I told him to go back to the house, and he turned around, his head hanging down. Why didn't I bring him with me, why?

"*Hyung*, I'm here."

You must live, my little brother, you must stay alive. I'll come and get you. You just wait and see.

chapter 7

FOREIGN STUDENT

Half dreaming and reminiscing, I saw dawn coming through the unfamiliar window. It took me a while to reorient myself from Chestnut Grove to Los Angeles. I recalled the three-day journey, starting with the airplane ride on Cathay Pacific from Seoul to Tokyo, followed by the Pan Am flight to Honolulu. Then the excitement of seeing Los Angeles from the air, the straight boulevards that stretched forever. Outside the window, unfamiliar birds chirped. With the new sounds and the new smells in my bedroom came the realization that I was in Los Angeles now, half way around the world from Chestnut Grove.

What now?

The question was an easy one to answer. I needed money, first of all. To register at the University of Oregon and to live on during school, I needed money. The $50 dollars from selling *kim* in Tokyo wasn't going to get me very far. For now I didn't have to worry about where to sleep, thanks to Hung Sa Dahn. My meals were taken care of as well. Mr. Ha's wife (Se-mun Choi) prepared the meals for me, and I walked to the Ha's to eat everyday. She didn't expect any money, and I couldn't pay her anyway. I gave her a big bundle of the *kim*, and she became excited. She had not seen Korean *kim* for ages, and it made her homesick.

Consulting with Mr. Ha, he agreed that I would need money during school. He took me to restaurants around town to see if they needed busboys even though I had no idea what busboys did. But getting hold of a busboy job wasn't all that simple. Everywhere we went to, they wanted my social security number, which I was not eligible for. My student visa did not allow me to apply for a social security number, therefore, there was no work for me. The job hunting went on for four days without success.

On the fifth day I went to Mr. Song's funeral, spending the day with Willie and Mary, Mr. Song's son and daughter. They became my life-long friends. Through them, I became acquainted with the man I never met, the angel who brought me to America.

After the funeral my job search continued. I finally landed a job in a coffee shop as a dishwasher and busboy. When a scruffy looking young man from the Orient walked down the street by himself, people naturally assumed that he was a busboy or a dishwasher, and I was. In the land where a conversation began with "How do you do?" immediately followed by "What do you do?" in search of a point of reference for an interaction, I was stumped for words most of time. I didn't know what to say because I couldn't speak a word of English. They just assumed I was a dishwasher, which was fine with me. It didn't particularly bother me because first, I was indeed a dishwasher, and second, I was happy to have a job.

Mind you, I had to learn the trade on the job because I saw dishes for the first time in my life. In Korea people use bowls for everything: rice bowls, soup bowls, smaller, shallow bowls for vegetables and things, and tiny bowls for sauces. Forks? They were new to me also, along with butter knives, steak knives, teaspoons, soupspoons, serving spoons. Why do they have so many eating tools, I remember asking myself, but I had no time to dwell on the cultural difference. Washing those metal contraptions paid for my food and my tiny room with enough money left over for tuition.

As I said, I was happy to have a job, although things weren't all that rosy all the time. In my rush to do the job well and quickly, I dropped the dish tray one day. BAM, CLANK, CRASH, the broken dishes, the forks, the spoons, glasses, the cups, and the dirty water flew everywhere, drawing stares from customers, the waiters and the boss. The world halted right then: he'll kill me. The boss rushed over. He told me to bring a mop. I ran to the janitor's closet and grabbed a broom and ran back. I didn't know what he meant by a "mop," only guessing that the situation called for a broom and that the boss had wanted me to bring the broom. I was wrong. The boss repeated, "mop, mop," and handed the broom back to me. I turned around and ran back to the janitor's closet and grabbed the long stick with what looked like the pieces of rope tied at the end of the stick and ran back to the boss. The boss nodded and made a motion to mop up the mess, and I mopped and picked up all the debris as quickly as I could. All the time, I was think-ing, he'll kill me, he is going to fire me, how am I going to pay for all this mess? To my surprise, the boss didn't fire me. Instead he said, "don't worry, get back to work," patting me on the shoulder.

I learned two things that day: I learned what mop meant and that Americans appreciated hard workers. The boss was willing to forgive me for dropping a tray because I was a hard worker. I never took breaks (well, mainly because I didn't know what they were) and I never let dirty dishes pile up anywhere, not in the sink, not on the countertop, and never on customers' tables. I figured that the only thing I had going for me was to hustle, nothing else, and the hustle made up for the lack of language and experience. I did not drop another bus tray.

My first summer in America ended, and it was time for me to register at the University of Oregon for the fall semester. The boss hated to see me go. He wished me well and told me that I could work in any one of his thirteen restaurants any time I came back to Los Angeles. I took his remark very seriously. The vote of confidence from the first American employer touched off my own sense of confidence in the most infectious way. I politely said thank you, but I was screaming inside *I can make it in America!*

Sue understood my elation over the seemingly insignificant remark. She knew where I came from and how I got there. "Anytime you want to work, I have a job for you." Those were the words that I would always remember, especially through the tough times in school and in business. Success followed hard work without fail, and it was just that simple. Knock and keep knocking, and doors will open for you.

With some money saved, I looked forward to going to Eugene, Oregon, and getting back to studying physics. At the same time I felt ambivalent about leaving Los Angeles and all the people that made me feel at home.

When I wasn't working, I visited the folks at Hung Sa Dahn, and Helen Ahn, the wife of Dosan Ahn Chang Ho. She was the kindest woman I ever met. At 72, she was sharp as a tack, always interested in the new students like me. She thought I would need a heavier blanket for Eugene and she made a quilted blanket with her own hands, which made me feel special. I used it until I got married five years later. She also taught me a great deal about Dosan, the things I never knew before.

She showed me the letters Dosan had written to her. She had saved all of his letters ever since they came to San Francisco together in 1902, beginning with the letters from Riverside, California to San Francisco when his work took him to Riverside. Because of his work as a leader in the independence movement he spent more time away from home. He wrote letters from Shanghai, Manchuria, Russia, Germany, England, New York, Chicago, Hawaii, Australia, Hong Kong, Mexico, and from the Japanese prison.

She was particularly fond of the letter that began with, "To my Helen, the one I love," which she read aloud to me. I had known Dosan to be a man of high morals and lofty ideals and I never thought of him as a man who would tell so openly and freely that he loved his wife. She showed me the warm side of Dosan, and I felt privileged.

Mr. Han Shi-dae was another person who left an everlasting impression on me. He was a well-respected farmer and a wholesaler as well as the president of Hung Sa Dahn, and I sought his advice often. During one of the many conversations with him, I told him how I took advantage of the black market exchange rate in Korea. I expected him to praise me for the clever way I had manipulated the situation to my advantage. But instead his face turned stern and he scolded me mercilessly.

"What you did was deceitful and injurious to the country! How do you expect the country will progress if everyone cheats each other like that?"

I had nothing to say. That day I learned the lesson of my life as Mr. Han went on to explain the meaning of the common good. "Everything you do everyday at home, in school, or in business must be based on truth. Never lie, never cheat."

What I had considered a clever ploy was not something to be proud of. Mr. Han shocked me again by pulling out a crisp one hundred-dollar bill out of his wallet, a sizable fortune for a fifty cents-an-hour busboy. He said, "Here, take this and use it for your school books. Focus on learning the American system and put in honest work every day. Don't waste your time trying to go around the system."

I took the money without looking at him and murmured, "Thank you. I'll remember what you told me." And I did. Mr. Han's admonishment stayed with me throughout my life, and I owe him for whatever success I attained.

Mr. Cho Ohl-lim was another hard-working man from Reedley. Mr. Cho had escaped from the Japanese rule in Korea and left for China. Then he came to the U.S. to study in the 1930s, about the time when I was a toddler in Chestnut Grove, but he ended up working for the independence movement like many of the young exiles. He worked in farms and donated his wage earnings to the Korean independence movement. Never getteng married, he didn't have any children of his own. He treated me like his son, and I was very grateful.

More than anyone he was intensely curious about the war, my escape from the communist north, and my family. Hearing about my accounts of the events, he shook his head incredulously with tears in his eyes. As a devout Dosan disciple, he literally ate, slept, and lived for the independence of his native country, Korea. Although he was a quiet, unassuming man, his patriotism was genuinely fierce and he reminded me of my father.

The American victory over the Japanese Empire in World War II brought about the long-waited liberation for Korea. He thought he was going to fulfill his dream of seeing his homeland. By the time he was ready to make the journey home, the country was divided in two and his hometown in the North was out of reach. He couldn't go back to his hometown and to his family, which I knew something about.

I knew how he felt, though, only to a certain extent. His worn eyes and deeply tanned face told more sad stories than I could ever understand, as did his sagging shoulders, which were once strong and hopeful.

He was a good-looking man, neither tall nor short, and I met him at the Hung Sa Dahn house on my first night there.

He and I shared the room whenever he was in Los Angeles from Reedley. In the middle of the night I heard a crashing noise, and I turned on the light to find Mr. Cho hunched over holding his forehead. He had bumped his head against the post on his way to the bathroom in the dark. I guided the staggering man to the bathroom and cleaned out the bad gash on his forehead and bandaged it. He staggered to his bed and fell back asleep, or more likely, he slipped into a liquor-induced unconsciousness. As it turned out, the nighttime staggering was a routine for him, and it had been for quite some time.

The money that he used to give to the independence movement went for bottles now. He had no family and no hobbies other than getting together with several of his old bachelor colleagues and recollecting the glory days. They drank and talked about Korea every night and then they staggered home when the bars closed. My heart went out to the old man, who, despite his own state of mortification, tried to point me to the future—schooling, and the fruitful life yet to come. "Study hard and make something of yourself," he said repeatedly. I knew what he meant. I heard it so many times, from my father, my mentors in Korea, and now in America.

Just as I was beginning to feel at home in Los Angeles with all these people around me, it was time for me to leave for Eugene.

I sent ahead my arrival schedule to the school. Mr. Ha drove me to the Union Station near Chinatown, where I boarded the afternoon train headed for Oregon, about 1,000 miles north of Los Angeles. I was nervous about my first railroad trip in America, not knowing where Eugene was or what to expect. Mr. Ha tried to calm me down. He told me about the diner car and the bathroom, and I nodded, half listening half worried about the long trip. My last train ride in Korea had been a frantic one, running from the bombs and explosions not too far behind, and I suppose I was not totally convinced that the train would go where it was scheduled to go.

The train rolled lazily out of the station, and I relaxed a little in my own seat in the half-empty car. Soon the ocean came in and out of view, as the train chugged along the serene coastal route. And it dawned on me that I was not escaping from bullets and tanks, but I was headed to the University of Oregon to study. Then came the new worries. I worried about everything in those days. What if I couldn't make it at school? What then?

After dinner I dozed. I woke up whenever the train slowed into a station, wondering if it was Eugene. I reminded myself that the train wasn't due in Eugene until the morning. What if I flunk out, I thought and I dozed again as the train pulled out. Until the next stop. I dozed and slept like that all night, and the train pulled into Eugene station at daybreak shortly before seven.

Green fields and trees went on forever in the drizzly horizon with new smells and new sights that were quite different from Los Angeles, and I washed up quickly in the bathroom to calm my nerves. As I got off the train Dr. Kent greeted me, the cheerful Foreign Student Advisor from school. My first thought was, *Is there something wrong?* He shook my hand heartily like he was happy to see me and I surmised that there was nothing wrong and I breathed out easily.

He helped me load the luggage into his car, and he took me to his house for breakfast. He had no qualms in bringing home and feeding a stranger from a strange country. His openness and generosity reminded me of my parent's hospitality to the wayward travelers passing through Chestnut Grove. This time, I was the wayward traveler.

"I'm okay," I said, "I had breakfast on the train." Since he was so kind already, far more than I had expected, I didn't want to be a burden any more. Being at the receiving end of hospitality is so much harder than giving.

He looked at me as if to see whether I was just being polite in saying "I'm okay," or I was really full. He brought me an open-faced grapefruit. I had seen the grapefruit in bus trays only at this point, the spent shell with the pink meat squeezed out of it. But I hadn't eaten one myself. The juice flew everywhere on to my shirt and across the table, and I had a devil of time finishing the grapefruit.

After the breakfast Dr. Kent took me around the pristine campus while we discussed my curriculum. He also told me a story about a Japanese diplomat, Mr. Matsuoka, who had attended the University of 'Oregon. He studied law at the university during the late 1920s. Even though the U.S. and Japan were on friendly terms at the time, evidenced by the American financial backing for Japan in the Russo-Japanese war (1904~1905), the Taft-Katsura pact, and the active trading that followed through his tenure in America, the university town of Eugene was not hospitable towards him because of his race. No barber in town would cut his hair, and he had to drive three hours to Portland for a haircut each time he needed one. Dr. Kent said that the University sought to correct the situation because years later, Mr. Matsuoka returned to the United States as the Ambassador of Japan, this time only to make the historical announcement of severing the relationship with the United States on December 7, 1941.

In his announcement of severing the relationship after the Japanese armada attacked Pearl Harbor, Mr. Matsuoka denounced the U.S. and its policies. The University thought that the harsh wording in Mr. Matsuoka's speech arose from the bad impressions he had acquired while he was a student in Eugene. The University now encouraged students from Asia to attend the school, offering generous scholarships and assistance.

By this strange turn of history, I came to benefit from the new policy at the University, and with it came the new realization that circumstances do change with time and place. I wasn't sure that Dr. Kent knew about the Japanese domination in Korea, and the deep-rooted resentment, even hatred, that Koreans felt towards the Japanese as the result of the 36-year occupation. I wasn't about to tell him about the oppression and the atrocities which Hirohito and his men had committed. It would have been too long a story for Dr. Kent who was more interested in showing Eugene in a better light than Mr. Matsuoka had seen. I didn't think that he was interested in the distinction between a Korean and Japanese.

We continued to talk about my studies in physics at the University, and I told him that I was worried about my ability to keep up with the work because of my English. He told me not to worry and that he arranged a roommate for me at the dorm. My roommate majored in education, specializing in teaching English for people like me. The arrangement worked out very well. I learned English, and my roommate practiced his teaching skills, a "win-win" situation.

On the first Sunday after I arrived in Eugene, I went to the First Presbyterian Church near the dormitory. The big and airy church was filled with men in good suits and women in Sunday dresses and hats, as well as the children in their Sunday clothes. They all seemed happy and peaceful without a worry in the world, a state of mind I was not familiar with, and I was very impressed.

Back home people didn't smile in or around the church. There wasn't much to smile about, really. In Seoul, people went to church to pray for food and to mourn for the lost family members, it seemed. And in America people said "Hello" to each other, exchanging pleasant smiles, shaking hands and hugging. I didn't know what the Americans prayed for, but from the looks of the congregation, I guessed that they did not need to pray for food because they appeared very strong and healthy.

The disparity between the two countries was quite striking, and I tried to make sense of the way God, the same God, brought so much wrath upon Koreans while He blessed Americans with wealth and happiness.

The usher guided me to a seat near the center aisle, and I sat down. The minister began his sermon, and my thoughts drifted back to the rabbit shaped peninsula far, far away across the Pacific, where father was buried and mother with the little ones wondering whether I was alive. *Will I ever see her again? Is my brother alive?* The minister's voice echoed in the church but I didn't hear or understand a word he said. A sudden fit of tears invaded me from within. The quiet tears flowed helplessly even though I closed my eyes tightly with my head down. I don't know what triggered it, maybe the thought of sitting in a church in a town that looked like a paradise. Maybe I finally relaxed and all the tension turned to tears pouring out of me. Whatever the reason, I felt totally cleansed after the good cry.

After the service the Pastor came up to me and asked me

if everything was all right. I shook his hand awkwardly, embarrassed for the way I wept in public. He held my hand for a long while and tried to talk to me, but I just wanted to get away as quickly as possible. He wasn't about to let me get away that easily. He called over his assistant Pastor and asked the younger minister to take me home. I declined profusely for the kind offer, not wanting to attract more attention to me. But the Pastor and the assistant Pastor were far too persistent, and I agreed in the end to go with the assistant Pastor. He took me to his home and we watched football on television while his wife prepared lunch. The assistant Pastor picked me up every Sunday from then on for church service, then lunch and football games. I did not cry in church again.

The following week the school opened for the orientation, registering for classes, and so forth. To my delight Dr. Kent introduced me to some Korean students, ten or so all together, and they filled me in on campus life. They told me about the College Entrance Examination, a difficult test that everyone had to take in order to gain admission to the school. I was alarmed to hear about the entrance exam. I told them that I had been admitted to the University already. I had the letter of admission and the financial assistance. I was living in the dormitory with a roommate already. They insisted that the test was a part of the requirements, and I was scared. I scared so easily then.

As it turned out, my new Korean friends were misinformed. The test they referred to was not an entrance examination per se. It was merely a placement test to determine the level of academic achievement and to determine which courses I needed to take. Boy, was I relieved to find that out!

Knowing that the placement test was not a live-or-die event, I took the test in stride, answering the multiple-choice questions as best as I could. The math portion was easy as the questions dealt with basic algebra, but the English part gave me sweaty palms. I didn't have any idea how well I did. I walked away thinking that I had a long way to go in English.

I registered for 12 units, the minimum amount of class units required to maintain the full-time student status. Calculus and differential equations were relatively easy because I had studied the same subjects in Korea. I spent most of my time studying English, spending many late nights flipping through the dictionary over and over. After a while I felt comfortable about school, juggling my hours between studying and working at the dormitory cafeteria for books and spending money.

There wasn't enough time for sleep though, and I even wrote an essay in the English class about my dire wish to sleep as long as I wanted. Everyone in the classroom laughed heartily when I read it aloud and some even expressed sympathy.

Despite the lack of sleep, my life on campus was good. I was on a steady course now. My struggles were less frantic and more predictable, therefore manageable.

I even found time for the Sunday evening "Korean" meal at an off-campus apartment of Korean friends. Every Sunday evening, we gathered at the apartment for the cook-off. In a huge pot we cooked beef chunks in boiling water with salt and heaps of hot chili pepper. We feasted on steamed rice and the concoction we called hot meat soup until we couldn't eat any more.

chapter 8

INDIANA BOUND

Summer came and I headed back to Los Angeles and the Hung Sa Dahn house on Catalina Street. Mr. Ha picked me up at the Union Station and he was so happy to see me, he made me feel like his son coming home. As much as I enjoyed Eugene and the gracious hospitality, I still felt like a visiting guest. There was no substitute for speaking Korean to familiar faces. Or home cooking. I was very glad to see Mrs. Ha, indeed. I wolfed down cabbage kimchi, sautéed spinach and bean sprouts that crunched just so as I sank my teeth into them. They wanted to know everything about Eugene, and I told them in between mouthfuls of food I had craved for so long. After dinner, I was back in my Hung Sa Dahn homestead, unpacking and planning for the summer. I thought of the owner of the diner who told me, "You can work for me anytime you're in town."

Next day I caught the Red Line to the coffee shop and said hello to the restaurant owner. The old boss was happy to see me and put me to work right away. He also raised my rate to seventy-five cents an hour, which made me a very happy worker. I whistled as I worked, clearing off the tables like lightning, scraping the dirty dishes, stacking them in the dishwasher along with the cups in the cup rack, the glasses in the glass rack, and the silver ware in its own rack. I pushed the button to start the steaming dishwashing machine. The machine whirled and I took the dried glass rack to the waiter's station, then the clean coffee cups and saucers. I took the clean dishes by the cooking station and brought back dirty pots and pans. I soaped, scrubbed and rinsed pots and pans as quickly as possible, for the cooks liked to have the utensils handy all the time especially when the order tickets were stacked up one after another in a row. I made sure that the cooks had everything they needed, clean dishes, pots and pans. They liked working with me. So did the waitresses. I kept the glass trays, the cup trays and the silverware trays full, and the waiters never ran out of clean glasses, cups and silverware. As I said, I cleaned the tables as soon as the customers left, which meant that the waiters could seat the new customers that much quicker. The table turn-over rate was noticeably better when I was on duty, and the waiters shared their tips with me without fail. When things were slow I cleaned everything in sight, the floor, the walls, the tables, the prep room, the walk-in cooler, the bathrooms, and by closing time the entire restaurant was squeaky clean.

I managed to save around $300 that summer, which was enough to last through the following fall semester and the next. After another year, I completed all the requirements for a physics degree.

I needed to make a decision whether I should continue with physics and pursue an advanced degree. I thought that the only thing I could do with physics was teaching—the job market for a physics major was limited. Teaching didn't appeal to me much. I felt that there was no money in teaching, and I sought after a more lucrative profession. I talked to everyone about my dilemma, and the general consensus was that the engineering profession paid better than physics.

So I went on a search for an engineering school. The University of Oregon didn't have an engineering school then, and I looked into other schools across the country, including Oregon State University in Corvallis. Of all the schools, Indiana Institute of Technology (I.I.T.) seemed most reasonable in terms of the academic requirements and the tuition. I especially liked it because I.I.T. emphasized the math and science courses.

Other universities required a lot of units in the general subjects involving extensive reading and writing in English in order to acquire an engineering degree, which would have been torturous for me. My aim in life was to avoid pain and suffering as much as possible and I applied to I.I.T., which accepted me promptly. They also gave me credit for the units from Yonhee (Yonsei) University and I could earn an engineering degree in four semesters. This was a bonus for me. My goal was very specific. I wanted an engineering degree in the most expeditious way so that I could make a good living, be it in Korea or America. I believed that the engineering degree would be my ticket out of poverty.

I had enough knowledge and experience in poverty, in fact, I was a Ph.D. in that subject. So I can say confidently that poverty is not a good thing. It is a disease, a state of mind that infects your entire being, your disposition, your outlook. Day and night all you think about is food. You go to sleep on an empty stomach, dreaming about a bowl of steaming rice. You try to recall the sweet aroma as you doze off in the dark.

Although I didn't grow up rich, I was fortunate enough to know that hunger was a temporary state. I believed that I'd be full again someday. That is an important piece of knowledge because it kept me going during my years as a war refugee and a starving student in Korea. As a student in America, I solved the food problem by working at the restaurant during the summer and at the dorm cafeteria while school was in session.

I was never hungry, thanks to all the hamburgers that came with the job. In between rushes of diners I wolfed down hamburgers for breakfast. I wolfed down another hamburger after the lunch rush, then after the dinner rush. My first lunch in America at the Honolulu International Airport, the strange looking concoction with two pieces of puffy round bread, became my main staple for four or more years. In terms of nourishment my life was simple.

What's for breakfast?

Hamburger.

What's for lunch?

Hamburger.

What's for dinner?

You guessed it. Hamburger.

I had more than my share of hamburgers, and I became sick of them. Yet I fed my body dutifully with hamburgers as though I fed coal into a stove. Like I said, hamburgers came with the job, free of charge, and that was good enough for me. I didn't worry about what and when to eat, which simplified my life immensely. I had other problems to deal with, like which field of engineering I was going to major in.

I.I.T. offered AE(Aeronautical Engineering), CE(Civil Engineering), EE(Electrical Engineering), and ME(Mechanical Engineering) curricula. I only had a vague notion about these fields, and at the first brush, I set my sight on Aeronautical Engineering because I wanted to do something unique. I wrote to Mr. Chu Yo-han in Korea for his advice on the matter, but I didn't get a reply. So I talked to the chairman of the AE department about my pending decision.

I asked Professor Benjamin Dow, "I don't know much about Aeronautical Engineering. I am from Korea and there isn't Aeronautical Engineering in Korea. So I'm thinking about going into the field and I would like to know what you think about that."

The aged professor with a crewcut nodded and replied, "Let me tell you how I became an aeronautical engineering professor and how I got to sit here with you face to face," and began telling me his story. He studied aeronautical engineering at Purdue University, he said. When he graduated there was only one place he could work. That was Boeing Company in Seattle. He wasn't too keen on going so far from home although he knew he didn't have much choice where he could go. Moreover, his wife strongly opposed the idea of going to Seattle as well. Many times, he said, he regretted having studied aeronautical engineering. He remained at Purdue and pursued the advanced degrees and ended up in the teaching profession. After he finished his story he asked me, "If you study aeronautical engineering, will you be able to use it in Korea?"

I answered, "Maybe not yet," recalling that there weren't many airplanes in Korea other than the military ones from the U.S., and that there was no Korean airline company.

"That's right. But it's more difficult to get a job in the U.S. because the specialty jobs in aeronautics are defense-related. And it's hard even for an American citizen to get a job in the industry without top clearance."

Listening to the professor, it occurred to me that I hadn't thought through the entire process. I needed a profession that I could rely on in Korea, in America or anywhere in the world for that matter. I decided aeronautical engineering was not right for me, even though I had been enthralled with the exciting technology. From studying physics I was very familiar with the theories behind flying, and with the understanding came the romantic notion about the sleek and graceful flying machines in the sky. With the professor's help, I brought myself down to earth and thought of building roads and bridges instead.

Roads and bridges were needed everywhere, especially in Korea, not to mention dams and electric power plants. I recalled the bombed out bridge in Pyongyang with all the people crawling on it and hanging on to it. What made America great was its excellent infrastructure, its roads, bridges, and the rail system. These were the things I could learn to build. There would always be a demand for engineers in this field and I would make a good living. With these thoughts in mind, I enrolled in the Civil Engineering Department of the small college in a sleepy mid-western town.

Autumn came early in Fort Wayne, Indiana, and my introduction to the civil engineering profession began with a surveying class, which took place outside in the fields around the campus. The fall colors were in full bloom, and the romantic notions I had for aeronautics faded as I delved into the science of surveying.

I thoroughly enjoyed the surveying class and I couldn't wait until we went outside to set up the tripod and fix the transit instrument on the tripod to look through the viewing scope with a cross hair. The class assignment was to map out the campus, its parcel description complete with streets, streetlights, underground gas lines, sewer line and manhole covers, power and telephone lines, buildings, and trees. I had never been more excited about class-work. The subject matter was real. I was dealing with things I could see and feel, not just the abstract theories in books.

In Eugene I had struggled with English, but I did not feel the pressure in Fort Wayne. I conversed easily with my classmates and professors. In addition to the surveying class, the curriculum went into steel structure design, concrete structures and wood structures. In every class, the professors stressed the practical application, not just the theoretical aspect. More than book learning, I enjoyed going out to the sites and seeing the structures take shape. I needed the exposure to the real world to understand the nuts and bolts: how and why the bridges, buildings, and roads were made the way they were.

A bridge was something I saw and crossed every day, but I had never paid attention to the huge mass of steel and concrete. A bridge was not just a bridge, but a carefully engineered and constructed structure with thousands of pieces of steel. Each piece of steel had a purpose and a name, I became intimate with them through books and field trips. We studied them all: suspension bridges, truss bridges, welded steel bridges, and concrete bridges.

After that, I saw more than just a massive hunk of steel when I crossed a welded steel bridge. I saw girders with web plates, top flanges, bottom flanges, cover plates, stiffener plates, and gusset plates. Inside I felt special as I became familiar with words like truss, chord members, braces, span, camber, tensile strength, compression strength, shear strength, bending stress, fatigue stress, moment connection, bolted connection, and all the ramifications that came with these words.

A bridge was not just a bridge any more. I shared special knowledge with the bridge-builders that designed, planned, and erected the roadway bridge or the railway bridge over a river or a valley to move people, cars, trains, trucks, and buses from point A to point B. I was on my way to becoming a member of the fraternity and I felt privileged.

My enthusiasm showed in my grades, and the professors began to notice me, even the president of the college, Dr. Archibald Keene. Dr. Keene and his wife were kind to me, inviting me to dinners and giving me a job to clean their house on weekends.

The Dean of Engineering, Professor Robert Rule was also very kind towards me. He was very popular among students because he was truly interested in the well-being of the students. He always checked on how I was doing in school and advised me on what I needed for my future. He was not only an engineering professor, but a teacher of life, and I always enjoyed talking to him freely.

With my graduation three months away, he asked me what I planned to do next. I told him that I didn't know for sure. I had no idea what I was going to do, whether to get a job or go back to Korea.

He asked me, "What do you want to do?"

I replied, "I want to stay in America and work as an engineer."

He said, "Then, that's what you should do."

I nodded but I didn't have any idea as to where and how to go about getting a job. During those days government agencies and corporations competed for graduate engineers, and the top graduates received many offers to choose from. It was a great time to be an engineer. The demand for engineers was huge and the supply was limited. The Soviet Union had launched the first satellite Sputnik into space, and President Eisenhower called for a massive government investment in science and technology. Engineers were in short supply. All my classmates had a job to go to, having been recruited during the school year. At the student union and at gatherings, my classmates shouted excitedly where they were headed: to the Corps of Engineers, GM, US Steel, and so on.

Despite the massive mobilization of the engineering manpower all over the country, I didn't have a job to go to and I felt left out. Dean Rule sensed this and wanted to do something for me. He also understood that most of these engineering jobs required U.S. citizenship, which I didn't have. Well, I didn't even have a social security number at that point, and the first question recruiters asked was, "Are you a U.S. citizen?"

So there I was, caught in a tough situation, and Dean Rule came to my rescue. He called a former student of his, now the County Engineer in Van Wert, Ohio. Dean Rule said into the telephone, "Norman, I have a new graduating engineer for you to meet. He needs a job and you need a person like him. I would like to bring him down to meet you. When is the best time for you?"

He hung up the telephone and smiled, taking off his glasses and rubbing the bridge of his nose. I looked at the big, kind man with a new sense of respect. It is more accurate to say that I was in awe. Did he just arrange an interview for me? I asked myself. I didn't believe what happened until the Dean picked me up in his car and we started out for Van Wert, about fifty miles east of Fort Wayne. I was a nervous wreck, not knowing what to expect at an interview for a professional job. Sure, I knew about interviews for dishwashing and bussing jobs. I had those down pat. I had a job waiting for me in Los Angeles, any time I wanted it in any one of the thirteen coffee shops. But an engineering job was more complicated than hustling bus trays.

Dean Rule sensed my nervousness and he tried to calm my nerves all the way down to the small Ohio town. He was very encouraging as usual. "Young," he said, "Relax. If I were a Korean, I would never be able to do what you've done."

I merely nodded, not knowing how to respond, just looking at the grain silos and the barns alongside the two lane country road. Harsh Midwestern winter had passed and there were signs of spring in the pastoral landscape all around, with cattle grazing in distant meadows. All I knew was that I had to get the job and I told Professor Rule, "I have to get the job."

"You will, you will. Try not to worry too much. I'll do all the talking to start with. Okay?" he said as we pulled up to the three-story brick courthouse on East Main Street near the junction of Conrail Railroad line and the Penn Central Railroad. Built around 1874, the tall courthouse was a typical building you can see at any small town, USA. I liked the buildings and the town atmosphere right away. The engineering department was in a remodeled warehouse behind the courthouse, and I straightened my necktie as we entered the office.

Mr. Norman Conn was a pleasant gentleman in his fifties, not as intimidating as I had imagined for a County Engineer, an elected office in Van Wert County. He chatted amiably with Professor Rule, and the informality between the teacher and the former student surprised me. They carried on the conversation as though they were two old friends rather than a teacher and a disciple. In my world a teacher was seated next to God Himself, and I wouldn't dare to venture towards the state of familiarity that I was witnessing. Yet it was obvious that they had high regard for each other with mutual respect and friendship.

After the small talk, Professor Rule got down to business and said, "I came along with Young because he has a great deal to offer. I know that you need help, and I also know that Young can help you. Young is smart and he works very hard, and I have no doubt that he will work out for you. He also needs your help. He wants to stay in America and work as an engineer and you can help him do that."

Mr. Conn turned to me and said, "I can sure use the help. Young, be here the day after graduation."

chapter 9

INTERN

On May 29, 1959, I graduated from Indiana Tech, having earned a civil engineering degree. My long quest for an education had finally become a reality, and I was the happiest man alive. My classmates and I celebrated late into the night, singing and hollering in between gulps of beer. I didn't drink, so I joined the cheer with a mug of soda in my hand.

Nuts, bolts, screws, gears!

Rah Rah engineers!

Three cheers, free beers!

Rah Rah engineers!

On June 1, 1959, I reported to work at Van Wert County engineering office, three days after the graduation. I had piled everything into the old clunker of a car and drove into town the day before and found a small apartment near the courthouse. I became somewhat of an attraction in town. Van Wert folks had never seen an Asian before and I got the dubious honor of being the first person of Eastern persuasion they had laid their eyes on. Some folks welcomed me enthusiastically, especially the high school students, who asked me for autographs. I signed my name with equal enthusiasm, feeling a bit embarrassed about the unexpected attention.

All in all, I enjoyed my three years in Van Wert. The people were wonderful, and I learned a lot working for Norman Conn. Mr. Conn was well respected around the County, known for his acumen in surveying skills and his fairness in dealing with property disputes. He was a popular elected official and no one challenged him for the seat for many terms. There were four other engineers in the office plus fifty or so field maintenance crew out on job-sites all over the County.

I liked Joe, the old-time surveyor, who continuously chewed on a fat cigar. We were out on a job one day and he watched me set up a transit instrument. It took me thirty minutes to plumb the tripod and to level out the transit gun.

The gun wasn't perfectly level in all directions, and I kept adjusting the leveling nuts and readjusting them. He was watching me patiently the whole time. After a long while he couldn't take it any more and he hollered out half jokingly, "What did you learn in college?" and he proceeded to teach me the proper way. After that, the phrase became a running joke directed towards me, a rookie just out of college. There was a lot to learn and I asked a lot of questions even though the older engineers repeated, "What did you learn in college?"

Days and weeks went by, and as I became acquainted with the work I graduated from rookie status after several months. Norman assigned a County car to me, a black Chevrolet sedan, and I felt like a big shot around town. I drove it for work on weekdays going to job sites all over the county. Norman let me drive it on weekends as well, my old clunker finally having seen its last days after the perennial breakdowns. The old car spent more time in the shop than on the streets, and its condition turned for the worse after I crashed it into a ditch off of a gravel road one night.

On Sundays I drove the county car to deliver the tape-recorded copies of the sermon to those who couldn't make it to the service at the Presbyterian Church. My main chore at the church was to bring the sermon to the elderly and the ill and to see if they needed anything. Life was good in Van Wert. Having grown up in a small village, I took to small town life rather easily. I especially enjoyed summer barbecues—the juicy steaks, sausages, and even hamburgers and hot dogs. I liked biting into fresh ears of corn covered with dripping butter.

But then, I still missed rice and kimchi terribly. I also missed Korean company, being able to speak freely without worrying about pronunciation and grammar. I drove to Fort Wayne now and then to meet up with four or five Korean students at Indiana Tech. We got together on Friday nights and made rice and the meat soup concoction with a lot of chili powder. I heard about Chicago during one of these get-togethers and I decided to visit Chicago and the Korean community there. Besides missing rice and kimchi I missed female companionship and I was ready to travel anywhere to meet and socialize with Korean girls.

Driving the County car all the way to Chicago was out of the question. Norman was gracious enough to let me take the car to Fort Wayne, but Chicago was a different story. Late October or early November of 1959, I went down to the Chevrolet dealer and bought a brand new Belair for

$2,000, putting down $200 for the down payment. I felt like a king. That was the beginning of my weekly trek to Chicago, 150 miles one way.

That's how I met Sue, during one of these visits. After we began dating, the Chicago trek became a routine, and I couldn't wait to get on the road on Friday afternoons, every Friday for a year. Like I said, Lakeshore Drive was our favorite spot, and it was there that we spoke about the future, sharing our futures together. I proposed to Sue on one rainy evening, and we didn't notice that the rainwater had come halfway up the wheels. We were talking and talking and suddenly a flashlight shone through the car window. We looked up and saw a policeman standing in the rain and peering into the car. I rolled down the window, and the policeman said, "The water is halfway up the wheels. It's not safe to stay here. We'll pull you out of here."

I looked down and sure enough, the water was about to come through the door. The policeman hooked the chain around the bumper and pulled. As they pulled, I steered the car carefully away from the flooded parking lot to the higher grounds. Afterwards the policeman unhooked the chain, and I thanked him profusely. He left, and Sue and I laughed good and hearty, saying, "What a disaster it would have been if the policeman hadn't come by!" We celebrated the narrow escape and our good fortune and went back to the business at hand, the promise for the future. She said yes, and I said yes, and I was no longer an orphan on the run.

We got married on November 25, 1961, and the wedding was somewhat of a social event for Van Wert with Reverend Robert McCochran presiding. The local radio station and the newspaper covered the wedding, and many people turned out for it, among whom were the County Supervisors, the judges, the Sheriff, and Norman and the staff from the office. One of the judges said, "I've never seen a Korean wedding before and I wanted to see it."

Dr. Archie Keene, the President of Indiana Tech, came to the wedding with his wife. Dr. Keene gave away the bride, and he was the picture of a proud father with Sue walking down the aisle by his side. As they walked to the tune of the wedding march song, Sue drew ooh's and ah's from the pews all around. I realized then that all the town folks turned out to see her, the beautiful oriental bride that I brought home from Chicago. Now that I think back, hell, they didn't care about me at all. But then why should they? They saw me every day and they knew who I was. They just wanted to see why I raced out of town like a bullet every Friday afternoon, that's all. And boy, did they get an eyeful! Now they knew why I made the crazy commute to Chicago come rain or shine.

As she marched down the aisle my stomach churned like never before. The whole thing was unbelievably fine, but then I was riddled with worries, my usual reaction to just about any situation or event. This time, my mind raced with new worries of becoming a husband, and the responsibilities of becoming a head of household. How am I going to support our family? She came closer and I saw how beautiful she was and all the worries evaporated like magic.

At the church reception everyone lined up to hug Sue and give her a kiss. All the men shook my hand and slapped my back and said, "You're one lucky man!" The women were more congenial in wishing for happiness for both of us. My landlady was the happiest person at the reception. She was the mother for both of us as well as being the host for the reception, bless her heart.

Then there was the matter of the paperwork. In between cake and coffee, the Minister signed the marriage license, the Judge witnessed it and handed it over to the County Recorder, who then put it in his coat pocket for the recording on Monday morning. We also needed to make a petition for Sue's visa as Mrs. Young Paik, and the same Judge signed the application form for her right there at the same table. With the efficiency of a small town all the paperwork was taken care of just like that, and we moved on to the next topic. Everyone wanted to know where we were going for the honeymoon, and I told them of our plan to stop first at the Cleveland immigration office to drop off the papers for Sue's visa and then on to Niagara Falls. Ah, Niagara Falls, they chimed and nodded. *It's pretty cold up there this time of the year. Be careful where you're stepping.*

Back at home in Van Wert, life took a turn for the better. For one thing, my weekly trip to Chicago came to an end, thus saving all kinds of money. Between paying rent, the car payment, the gasoline, and the traveling expenses, I struggled every month even with the respectable engineer's salary. Sue took charge of all the financial matters and strangely enough, we did just fine. She was a nut on saving money, money for a house and money for the family in the future. She wanted to get rid of the car even, and I put my foot down, no, even though she had a point in saying that the car made very little financial sense.

I had a thing for cars; a nice car made me feel wonderful. On the other hand, Sue thought that a car should provide transportation, no more. This difference between us would come up again later whenever I wanted to buy a nice car. For now we kept the blue Chevy Belair, my pride and joy, and we went on with our lives as the first Korean couple in Van Wert, Ohio.

At work my responsibilities increased, I had finished the internship period and the training period. By the end of my 3-year tour at the County Engineer's office, I learned a great

deal about engineering and I was ready to move on. Sue and I talked about Los Angeles often. I talked about Los Angeles at work all the time and everyone knew that we would move to Los Angeles and settle there alongside my family from Hung Sa Dahn.

When I received a permanent visa from the Office of Immigration and Naturalization Service, we packed up all of our worldly possessions in the car and we headed west for Los Angeles.

chapter 10

ENGINEER

Mrs. Wiley Kerns, our landlady and the hostess for our wedding, hugged Sue and me, and cried. We were her children, who were about to venture away from home. The kind widow of a former County Supervisor made sandwiches for us and packed a cooler with drinks and fruits. "Don't forget to write," she said over and over. "The minute you get to Los Angeles you write to me."

"We sure will," we said, "As soon as we get settled, you come to California to see us."

"Yes, I will. And you drive very carefully, Young, and take good care of Sue."

"Yes, ma'am," I said and I promised her that I would drive nice and easy because Sue was pregnant with our first child.

With the tearful good-bye, Sue and I headed west, leaving

behind the fond memories of Van Wert, Fort Wayne and Chicago. It was late summer, and I wished that I had bought the air conditioning package with the car as we drove through the mid-western heat. We kept our windows rolled down, feeling free and full of anticipation for the new life that awaited us in Los Angeles, and the sultry heat didn't bother us too much—in the beginning, that is. As we passed by Chicago then drove on to St. Louis along Route 66, we stopped frequently to cool off the car and ourselves. I realized then that air conditioning was not a luxury but a necessity, especially when you had a pregnant wife on a cross-country trip with you.

We averaged about 500 miles a day. I wanted to go faster because I was anxious about finding an apartment and finding a job, but we couldn't fight the heat. We stopped in Oklahoma, Texas, New Mexico, and in Nevada. On the fifth day we entered California. I saw the "Welcome to California" sign and I was one happy fellow.

We stopped in San Bernadino and called Mr. Ha at the Hung Sa Dahn office. He was happy to hear from me and he told me how to get to the apartment he had arranged. "Go to West Boulevard Apartments on West Crenshaw in Los Angeles," he said.

THE DO OR DIE ENTREPRENEUR

We drove to the West Boulevard Apartments in Baldwin Hills area and entered the one-bedroom apartment next to Mary Song's, and so began our life in Los Angeles. The first thing we wanted was kimchi. We went to Daedong market on Normadie and we stuffed ourselves with kimchi for the first time in years and we forgot all about the long trip.

Next day I went to an employment agency and filled out an application. They arranged an interview with Soule Engineering Company right away. My interview with the big boss went very well. He was from Ohio originally and he was familiar with Van Wert County. I showed him the blueprint copies of my work from Van Wert on the county buildings and the bridges, and he hired me right away at $600 a month salary. That was quite a jump from the $350 I had been getting in Van Wert, and we were convinced then that we had made the right move.

It was a good start for the new family. I jumped into my new design engineering job with two feet, trying to come up to speed in the private sector as quickly as possible. I was a little nervous about the new arena in the commercial setting although I was confident about my steel design capability. As usual, I was the first one to arrive at work, and the fellow workers and the supervisors appreciated my dedication to the job. For this dedication, they rewarded me with more work, and soon, I was producing more design drawings than anyone in the office.

I didn't mind being the busiest man in the office because I felt that I was learning a lot and I was accumulating my skills inventory. But after a while I found myself in a "pigeon-hole" as the quiet Asian engineer who cranked out drawings like mad, the guy with the fast pencil and the meanest slide rule in the West. I was no different from a sweatshop worker locked in a cubicle with tons of material to sew, head down and coming up for air only once in a while. To put it simply, I felt like a technological coolie and I didn't like it.

In a corporate world, perception was everything, and I began my career at Soule as a small Asian guy with a language problem, who sat in a corner saying "yes" to everything. And they came at me every day with things like "Young, I need this drawing right away," or "I need this information right away," or "Forget what he told you, just move this beam over here," or "This is the way we do it around here."

I did not feel that I was a part of the team. In Van Wert, I felt like I was a part of the team. Mr. Conn and the rest of the engineers in the office and in the field wanted me to understand what was going on and they took time to explain why. At Soule, I expected the same thing. I wanted to be part of the action. I wanted to participate in the planning process. I wanted to talk about the scope of the project, the best way to design and build a warehouse or a factory. I wanted to follow up on the construction phases to make sure that the beams, the trusses, and the column were put together correctly. But they didn't want me to get involved with the actual business process. They wanted me to stick to the drafting board, run the numbers and crank out the drawings. My supervisors went as far as to tell me point blank, "We don't want you to talk to the customers. You just design the structure the way we want and do what we tell you."

Well, that was the wrong thing to tell a young engineer who was truly dedicated to saving money for the company. Perhaps they didn't know that I was always trying to find better and cheaper ways. In the office most of the engineers simply followed the procedures from past projects and the old design manuals without looking too deeply into new and different ways. In general, they were satisfied with the results that were "close enough," or "good enough."

Needless to say, I was frustrated on many levels. I suppose I could have gone along with the tide, put in my eight hours every day and take the easy way out. But I wasn't made that way.

Sue took the brunt of my frustrations as I continually grumbled about the stressful conditions at Soule, the waste I saw, the way they treated me, and how I missed Van Wert. Sue sympathized with me and she wanted me to start a business, a store maybe. I thought about that too, but I didn't want to throw away the years of my education and training as an engineer. So I gritted my teeth and stayed on at Soule, taking all the crap every day.

Thank God for Marilyn, our first child. After she was born, I was able to put up with the daily grind. She was a joy to come home to. I rushed home every day to hear her call me "Daddy," "*appa*" in Korean, and all my troubles went away.

Meanwhile, I stuck by my guns at work. I kept on challenging my co-workers and supervisors with money-saving ideas. This required extra effort and extra time, and they noticed that I was willing to give them these two things, while others were happy with the status quo. Such an approach put me in a unique class in the company, you might say. I found a way to survive my "pigeon-hole" and all the frustrations that went with it. Slowly, I made a reputation as the guy who liked tough problems and I ended up with the projects that no one else wanted to tackle.

Four years into Soule, a tough problem landed on my desk. With the advent of the Viet Nam War, Soule became extremely busy with the RFQ's (Request for Quotation) from DOD(Department Of Defense) for building quarters, hangars, and warehouses in Viet Nam. They wanted a building system that was easy to transport and assemble in the jungles and yet strong enough to withstand bombing.

Conventionally, the structural components like beams, columns and braces were pre-assembled and pre-welded in the Soule shop and shipped out to the job-site, where the welders joined together the pre-assembled parts. But the conventional methods did not work in Viet Nam where they didn't have much welding equipment or skilled welders to assemble the components. They could have shipped all the necessary equipment and manpower, but that would have taken too much time and money. They wanted a system that they could put up in a hurry and with little skilled labor. The biggest problem was the connecting method for joining the beam to the column and the corners where the roof and the wall came together. The usual "welded knee brace" would have taken many weeks, time they didn't have.

Basically, what they needed was a huge Erector Set, like the popular children's toy, made up of assorted sticks that can be inserted into round disks with holes, thus creating a structure. About that time, Bethlehem Steel Corporation and the U.S. Steel came out with the new high-strength bolts, and I thought that a bolted knee system would be a good application. The other engineers didn't think much about the idea because the high-strength bolts were new and untried. They were still stuck on the welded knee system, and they weren't about to go along with my idea. I designed a bolting pattern that looked like the lugs for mounting wheels on a car and showed them the calculation I made.

The numbers worked, I said, and I made a case for the ease of transporting the components and the quick installation. "All you need is the torque wrench. You don't need a welding machine and the power for it. You can train anyone to use the wrench."

They had never seen anything like that before, and they hemmed and hawed for a long time. But they didn't have anything better so they decided to send the proposal to DOD with my design, called "Paik's Knee" after my last name. To everyone's surprise, DOD accepted the proposal, and "Paik's Knee" became the standard for the military buildings in Viet Nam. Looking back, I had a leg up on everyone else. I knew about the war conditions from personal experience. I had seen what bombs could do to steel bridge girders, to beams and to steel tanks. I also knew that, in a war, time was of the essence. Every second, every minute would work for you or against you, in the matter of life and death. In designing "Paik's Knee," I can say that I made the best of my wartime experience.

Once the DOD approved the design, they bombarded Soule with purchase orders. We became busier than the swarming bees, churning out shop drawings in the design office while the production crew cranked out the steel parts in the shop around the clock.

That was the turning point in my engineering career. "Paik's Knee" became a common word around the office, and my assistant made a caricature of me holding a human knee section in one hand and a slide rule in the other, and hung it on the wall. I still have the cartoon on my wall. The company raised my salary too, but it was peanuts compared to the millions they raked in from my design. Nevertheless, I was happy about the raise and the promotion to Senior Engineer.

My bosses treated me with more respect after "Paik's Knee." They asked for my opinions in planning sessions and they listened. I was no longer the quiet Asian engineer in the corner for people to dump mundane projects no one wanted to do. Like magic, my lack of language skills was no longer a liability for the company. Now they wanted me to talk to customers. They even sent me to Korea in 1968 to survey the potential market there.

chapter 11

SALES ENGINEER

The "Paik's Knee" put me on the map as a capable engineer. I'd come a long way since I struggled with setting up a transit gun on the tripod in Van Wert as an intern, and the good-natured ribbing I took from the old timers—"What did they teach you in college?"

My commute to Soule Steel in South Los Angeles became much easier in my new car, a Chevy Malibu. I was the father of two children now, Marilyn and Nelson, six and five years old, respectively. They were kindergartners, going to school in Lomita, about ten miles south of Los Angeles. They were growing up fast and healthy, and I couldn't ask for more. As they grew though, my worries grew as well. I was looking ahead to their college years and I worried how I was going to send them to college and so forth. The new house in

Lomita took a chunk of my salary every month, and I couldn't see us saving enough money to send them to good schools later.

I was born to worry. I never ran out of things to worry about, like staying alive during the Korean War, surviving as a lone refugee, making it in America as a student, and now trying to make the mortgage payment for a suburban house and sending the kids to college. They were kindergartners then, and already, I was worried about their college education. At this rate, I had another eleven years to worry until they went to college. Yes, I took my job as a father very seriously, and that meant I worried myself to death.

My job at Soule was going well. I graduated from the sweatshop and moved on to bigger and better things, going to the staff meetings and the meetings with customers. My responsibilities grew, bringing in a lot of projects and managing them to the finish. The company was making a lot of money because of me, but my salary didn't grow as fast, and this became a new worry for me. My worries over the financial progress—or the lack thereof—peaked when I turned thirty-nine. Like the most people, I was concerned about turning forty, and I found myself thinking about what I had accomplished and what I was going to do in the future. I asked myself questions like, "Am I going to be a salary man forever?" My future rested with the company and my future there was limited, because there was no way in hell that they would make me an officer or a partner. I was a good engineer and they liked me, but I had to be realistic about my chances of advancement. I was destined to be an engineer until I retired, if I was lucky enough to last that long. Anything could happen to an employee. What if I got laid off? Where was I going to find a new job at age forty if I got laid off?

My concern wasn't only about job security, however. I wanted to be in control of my future. I wanted to be my own boss rather than leaving my future at the feet of the company president.

Sue and I went over these concerns, and she suggested that we start a liquor store, which would bring in more revenue than I was making. I wasn't sure about the liquor store, but I agreed to some kind of business and we took out a $10,000 loan from the bank. With the money in the bank, I felt better about the situation and we looked at many businesses while I continued to work at Soule. I was prepared to quit my job as soon as we found a suitable business, and I didn't care what happened to me at the office. I was less cordial with my bosses, talking off the top of my head. I bossed people around, treating them roughly. I even cussed a lot more than I used to.

Strangely though, my new attitude was perceived as new confidence, and they liked the way I conducted myself with the bosses and the customers. Damn, they thought I was a changed man. They smiled a lot more and patted me on the back like I was one of the boys. They gave me bigger projects, the important contracts with the cities, and they gave me a raise. I still shake my head at the way things turned out. Like I said, in corporate life perception was everything. I was doing the same thing all along, the only difference being the loudness in my voice, but I was more productive in the eyes of the corporate officers. Sue was puzzled too at the new development at work, saying that my engineering talent would be wasted on a liquor store no matter how lucrative it might be. She thought that I ought to do business that had something to do with engineering rather than a retail business. I decided to stay on Soule Steel for the time being and we gave the $10,000 loan back to the bank.

Meanwhile, my expanded role at Soule Steel took me outside the office more often, representing Soule's interest in meetings with various players in the business. I came in contact with Sumitomo Steel of Japan during this time, a contact that would develop into an important relationship later.

During the late 1960s and the early 1970s, Sumitomo Steel and other Japanese steel companies were trying to develop a market in the United States. At the time, the steel industry was controlled by American steel companies such as U.S. Steel and Bethlehem Steel, and it was unthinkable for Japanese steel companies to break into the market that was dominated by the steel giants. The common understanding around the industry was that the Japanese steel was inferior to the U.S. products, and there was no way that the Japanese companies could compete in the United States. The popular belief was that the Japanese companies used scrap metal to make structural shapes with, and no one touched the imported steel. (Truth was that the Japanese steel industry and the government had invested billions to modernize the steel mills.)

When I met the Sumitomo people, they were in the beginning stages of setting up a sales office in California. They told me how difficult it was to break into the steel market; they complained of the resistance, the false rumors and the general anti-Japanese mood among the potential customers.

They sought me out, they said, having heard about a well-known Asian engineer around Los Angeles. They didn't understand the resistance in the market because their products were made to American standards, AISC (American Institute of Steel Construction) specifications and so forth.

One day in 1969, I had lunch with the Sumitomo people. I told them that I was fifteen when I heard Hirohito's surrender speech on the radio in Korea and how I ran out and danced in the streets and celebrated the end of the Japanese colonization of Korea. And here we were, twenty-four years later, they were asking me, a Korean-born naturalized U.S. citizen, to buy their steel products for my projects in America. We marveled at the twists and turns of history, how far we had all come.

They understood my hatred for Japan and what it stood for in the past. They hoped that I didn't hold them personally responsible for the atrocities. I told them that I had no animosity towards them personally. After all, they were only kids at the time, I said. They were relieved to hear me say that. They were good people, highly educated and considerate, and I didn't have any problem with them.

I told them, "If the products test out I will recommend your products to the company. That's all I can do for you as the senior engineer."

They replied happily, "Thank you very much. We'll pay for the testing cost. Please conduct a test at your plant."

A few days later, they brought the sample beams, and we tested them. The quality was not as good as the domestic products, but it passed the standards. I asked about the price, and they said, "Whatever you think the price should be."

Their reply surprised me even though I understood that they wanted to break into the market no matter what the cost. Despite the favorable pricing, it wasn't easy to buy their products. At that time, our main suppliers were U.S. Steel and Bethlehem Steel, and we had to live with their edict, "If you go to any other supplier, we'll cut you off." It was pure bunk, but a terrible policy by the steel giants, threatening their customers with cutting them off. It went against all the principles of the free market system, but that was the reality of the monopolistic situation. Soule depended on U.S. Steel and Bethlehem Steel for supply, and without their supply, Soule would go out of business. U.S. Steel and Bethlehem Steel knew that they "had us by the balls," and we couldn't do anything about it.

In the end, we decided to use the Sumitomo products a small quantity at a time. I explained the situation to them and said, "Don't announce to anyone that we bought your products. Let's set the price at half the domestic price."

They agreed, "Whatever the condition is, it's fine with us."

So we began taking delivery from Sumitomo Steel, and our relationship proved to be a profitable one.

About the same time period a new company came onto the scene. Mark Crest Steel Company was formed, a partnership between Marubeni, a Japanese steel trading company and an American sales company. I had never heard of them before until a Mark Crest engineer came to see me at Soule. He introduced himself and asked me, "We are going to develop an automatic welding machine to produce welded beams. Can you design some prototype welded beams for us?"

They were asking me to do a consulting job for them, a moonlight job, and I said yes. I needed the money, and I saw a need for the welded beams. So after work and during weekends, I developed new welded beam sections that looked like the traditional I-beams, but were more efficient.

The traditional I-beams are made from steel ingots. An ingot is a large block of raw steel as big as a car or a refrigerator. The white-hot ingot goes through a series of rollers mounted on a track that looks like conveyor rollers. The rollers pound and roll the ingot and make it long, about 40 feet long, and pushes it into the next set of rollers that squash it into I-shape. It's a sight to see how the block of ingot turns into a beam, all the hot sparks flying and the pounding noise echoing in the huge plant that's bigger than ten Walmart's put together.

The welded beam starts out with long strips of steel. Instead of pounding the ingot into shape, the strips of steel are preset in the I-shape, two flange plates at the top and bottom and the web plate in between. The welding machine comes along and welds these plates together.

The end results are about the same between the rolled I-beams and the welded I-beams. The welded beam gives you more flexibility in terms of size, and you can custom-make the beams. You can't customize the rolled beams.

I liked the idea that you could customize the beams because there were many instances when the standard rolled beams didn't work, especially in the areas of mobile homes and manufactured houses. I gave Mark Crest my designs, and they developed the welding machine and produced the beams under my guidance as the welding expert.

For a year I worked full time at Soule while I consulted for Mark Crest part time. My income from Mark Crest grew as the welded beams sold very well, surpassing my salary at Soule. I quit Soule in mid-1971 and went to Mark Crest as the Vice President of engineering. Mark Crest was much smaller than Soule, and I had to wear a lot of different hats. Consequently, I learned a great deal about the commercial side of the steel business. I also learned that there was more money in sales than in engineering. What a revelation that was!

THE DO OR DIE ENTREPRENEUR

chapter 12

ON MY OWN

But then what did I know about selling? Do I call up a customer and say, "Hello, Mr. Smith, do you want to buy my beams?" How do I go about showing them what I have and get them to say yes and write me a check? If I wanted a hamburger I'd go to a hamburger shop. If I wanted a hammer I'd go to a hardware store. I'd pick out what I want and give them money and take it home. That's simple and straight forward like when I sold roasted chestnuts. I did okay with the chestnut stand, and what a vendor I was. What do I do with the beams, though? I couldn't stand in the street corner and yell like I did, "Buy my roasted chestnuts! Straight from Pyongyang!"

At first I accompanied the sales team to meetings with customers. My role as the Vice President of engineering was to provide technical support and answer the questions from the customers. The welded beam was a new concept to the industry, and the customers wanted to know what was different about our product. The salesmen would reply that our beams were stronger, lighter, and cheaper.

The customers asked, "Why?"

The salesmen deferred the questions to me and I explained that our beams were stronger and lighter because of the new design. I made sketches and wrote down numbers while I explained in halting English. "We made the flanges thinner by one-sixteenth of an inch. That's how we reduced the weight."

"Yes. But that makes the beam weaker."

"Yes, so we made the web taller. That gives us more sectional modulus. Because of the larger distance to the neutral axis."

The customers appreciated my explanation, and the pleased look on their faces made me feel good. They marveled at the simplicity, going on and on as though they discovered a long lost friend. They thought I was a genius, but all I did was take a closer look at the beam system that had been around for ages, that's all. I suppose I have a knack for looking at things, analyzing them and breaking them down to small components. Then I could take the small components and apply them to a new situation. In that sense, the new beam and its design process was no different from roasting chestnuts in coming up with a new way. I had come up with a new way of making roasted chestnuts and people loved my roasted chestnuts. I was a refugee in the middle of the war, and the chestnuts pulled me out of the streets, put me through school. Now they liked my welded beams, and I saw the parallel between the chestnuts and the beams. I didn't try to explain the similarity to anyone. They would have laughed at me and say, "What do roasted chestnuts have to do with welded beams?" But the analogy made perfect sense to me then and it does to me now.

There was one big difference between the two, though. As a chestnut vendor, I kept the profit, but as an engineer I took home my monthly salary. The profit went to the company and the owner. Following around the sales team and seeing how many tons of beams we sold and how much revenues "my" beams brought in, I was glad that my effort was paying off well. The company was doing well, yet I couldn't get rid of the bitter-sweet feeling that came with the success. My take-home pay was miniscule compared to the millions that my beams brought in, and that didn't sit very well with me. I wanted an explanation for the disparity and I watched the whole operation closely.

The owner of Mark Crest was a very capable salesman, and I learned a great deal about the commercial side of the steel business. I'll go as far as saying that he taught me everything about the steel business. Had I stayed on as engineer with a big company like Soule, I would have spent the rest of my career in the middle management level and I would not have seen the whole picture. Thanks to him, I learned how to listen to customers, the most important element in sales. You may be the smartest guy in the world with the most brilliant product, but if you don't know how to listen to your customer, you are the dumbest guy in the world. As far as an engineer goes, he or she is trained to dig into the technical aspect of the world. There is so much to know, and the more an engineer knows the better. An engineer is judged or graded on the level of expertise he achieves, and as a result, he has to be the smartest guy in his field. It is easy for an engineer to adopt an attitude that he was the foremost expert in his field, and such attitude is not necessarily bad. You need that sort of confidence to survive in the engineering field, but not the arrogance.

I was never arrogant about my ability. I didn't like to lose and there were many instances where I spent many hours and days trying to prove myself over the next guy, but I never felt that I knew everything. I was a good engineer, but there were plenty of engineers who were smarter than I was. From early on, I learned a lot of things by listening to other people and I never shied away from asking questions. If I didn't know something, I was never afraid to say, "I don't know." But I always followed up with, "But I'll find out for you." The customers appreciated the answer, and especially the follow-up call I made with the answer to the question. To be successful in sales business, you have to listen to what they want, that was the most important lesson I learned from Mark Crest.

Also, I learned about the importance of treating secretaries nicely. They can make you or break you. When I called on a customer and his secretary answered the telephone, I was cheerful and I took a personal interest in her not to fool her into thinking that I was a nice guy, but I genuinely felt that she was my customer, just as important as her boss. I made a point to remember her name and I said, "Hello, Miss Jones, how are you today?"

She rewarded me with, "I'm fine, thank you, Mr. Paik. How are you?"

I replied, "I'm fine. Running around crazy. So hot today. I hope you have air conditioning."

"Yes, we do, but it's still hot in here. Are you looking for the man?"

"Yes. Is he around?"

"Yes. He is cranky today, though."

"Okay, thanks for telling me."

That's how I greeted the secretaries, and my cheerfulness helped her day go better. Next time I saw her, I brought a small gift like a pretty handkerchief. I never once snapped at a secretary. I always treated a secretary like an important person because she was. At times I asked her to help me get the account, "With your help I think I can get the account." Next time I called, she recognized me and answered cheerfully, "Yes sir, Mr. Paik," and she made the business call much more pleasant.

I didn't always make a sale on the first call. I didn't try to overcome the resistance and "close" the deal by pressuring the customer. If I couldn't sell the beams to a particular client, I offered my engineering services and I continued the dialog with him. I always felt that it was more important to get to know the client first. That's what selling is about—find out what your customer wants and give it to him.

Of course I didn't learn these things overnight. It wasn't easy for me to take my ideas and express them to those who may or may not be familiar with steel and its strength properties. In terms of my personality, my background and training, I was a natural engineering type, quiet and unassuming kind of a guy, you might say, and I went to the school of hard knocks to learn the basic principles of selling.

After three years at Mark Crest, I became an accomplished salesman. Wearing two hats, one as the Vice President of Engineering and the other as a salesman, I worked harder than ever, running around like a madman, preparing designs, meeting customers, preparing quotes, answering technical questions, fielding customer complaints and solving staff problems. I put in long hours, which was nothing new, and the company prospered.

As busy as I was, however, I didn't feel satisfied. I should have been satisfied with my status as the head engineer in an up-and-coming company. I was there at the ground floor, helping them grow every year. I had a good salary at $30,000 a year in 1974, enough to feed a family of five with three growing children in a comfortable suburban home. In many ways, I couldn't ask for more. I had come a long way.

From those smelly refugee dumps to a big house with a carpeted living room and a kitchen with running hot and cold water, a garbage disposal, and a dishwasher. We had two bathrooms big enough that I could sleep in and clean enough to eat off the floor. No more flies, no more maggots. Also, I didn't have to worry about bombs coming down on my head, and the tanks and the bullets zinging by me and my family. We were living in peace in Southern California enjoying the life that I never dreamed of, and yet I felt incomplete.

After a long time I figured out what was nagging at me. The company was doing extremely well, but it wasn't mine. The product was my brainchild, and I did most of the work in making it grow, but I wasn't getting the credit. I was just an employee who worked like a dog day and night, and in the end I would have nothing to show for it. I wanted my own company.

I decided to go on my own.

chapter 13

PACO

Once I decided to go on my own, I worried. Whenever I was at a crossroad in life I always referred back to those war-torn days. Even though I had a comfortable life in America, I couldn't shed the feeling that it could turn into chaos. I had a wonderful childhood in Chestnut Grove, only to see my father lose everything, his life included, and I abandoned my family and ran for my own life. Life has many turns, and I was conditioned to worry about the unexpected. Worrying was a habit for me, and for many Koreans who experienced the war first hand.

When Marilyn came to this world, I was on cloud nine. Simultaneously, I was struck with a case of the worries and the enormity of the responsibility: "How am I going to feed her and send her to school and college?" The same worries hit me when my sons were born, but Sue was calm and confident at every turn in our lives.

She was more confident about my abilities than I was. I was having second thoughts and she said, "You have to start your own company. You have all the qualities of a business-man. You have the background and you know how to talk to customers. You know what they want and you shouldn't give your hard work away to someone else."

I argued, "Running a business takes more than just ability. You need capital, and what happens if it fails? The children are growing up, and it's not the time to take risks."

We had many arguments like this, Sue and I. And I am glad she prevailed over my reticence. She said, "Don't worry about money. I can do things to take care of the children. You have to decide what you really want. That's the most important thing."

If it hadn't been for my wife's encouragement, I wouldn't have gone ahead with my own company. As it was, Sue typed up a letter of resignation for me, and I carried it around with me for two weeks before I worked up enough courage to tell the company president. A few days before my summer vacation, I went into his office and I told him, "I am turning in my resignation. I plan to run my own business."

His mouth dropped as he asked, "What are you going to do?"

"It's not definite yet, but I'm thinking about the engineering services."

Before I finished the sentence, he stood up and yelled aloud, "Pack your things and get out right now!"

I had anticipated his objection to my resignation, but I did not expect the angry reaction from him. I gave him a short reply, "I understand," and went to my office and packed my private possessions and left.

One week later, I went to visit my friends at Soule. I had left Soule on good terms and I wanted to tell them about my new company.

"I'm thinking about a name for my company. How about calling it 'Paik Company'?" I asked them.

They said it aloud a few times and said, "It's not easy to say 'Paik Company'. How about taking the first two letters from your name, 'P' and 'A' and combine them with 'Co' from 'Company'? Call it PACO Engineering. That's easier to say than Paik Company."

I thought about that a while and agreed with them. PACO rolled off the tongue easier than the Paik Company, and I said, "It'll be PACO then."

Thus PACO was born, and we went out to lunch together to celebrate the humble beginning. At lunch I asked them if they had anything for me to do for them, and they said that they did need some engineering work done by a certified engineer with a license. Some projects required a professional engineer's stamp, which was no problem for me. I held an engineering license in the state of California as well as Arizona, Idaho, Nevada and Washington, and I said, "Sure, I'll be glad to help you, and I'll charge only a nominal fee for you guys."

Landing my first client, I went to see a mobile home man-ufacturer with whom I used to do business through Mark Crest. I offered them my engineering services, "I would like to do design work for you and whatever you need with the machinery or technology." To my delight, they came on board. I raced home to my office and pored over the speci-fications and the documents outlining the requirements. I laid out a clean sheet of drawing paper on the drafting board in the family room and knocked out the plans, the general arrangement drawing, the framing layout, and all the connection details including the types and sizes of the welds. In designing the structure and the components, I gave a lot of thought to the strength, the ease of fabrication, the economics, and the transportation of the units as though I was building my own home. Afterwards I went over the drawings and the calculations and checked them over and over. Next day or two I delivered the drawings and calcula-tions to the customer. Then I made my rounds to other cus-tomers. Some of them didn't have anything for me. I chatted about world affairs with them instead of beams. My goal was to sell them welded beams eventually, and I was more interested in keeping the dialogs going. It didn't bother me that they didn't have anything for me to do.

Some customers paid right away, and some didn't. Again, my long term goal of selling them beam products was more important and I didn't concern myself with the payments for my engineering service. I took the checks if they paid me. I continued to make the rounds during the day and I worked on my drafting board at night. The word got around about my engineering service, and customers began calling me. After a month or two I became quite busy. The pay was good, too, better than the salary I brought in from Mark Crest, and I became confident about PACO's future. The engineering service was taking off, and I concentrated on it for six months.

In the meantime, I kept in touch with Mr. Miahira from Fuji Manufacturing. Fuji Manufacturing was one of the three Japanese makers of welded beams, and Mr. Miahira sought me out initially because of my work in the light steel industry. He and I got on well together and we met many times to talk about doing steel business together. In the end, I offered to sell Fuji beams in the American market, and he welcomed the idea because of my familiarity with the industry.

We were all set to start on my role as a salesman for Fuji beams, but a problem came up with Mitsui Trading, the importing arm for Fuji Manufacturing, per the business arrangement. Mitsui Trading objected, "How can a small, new company like PACO sell the beams in the U.S. market?"

Fuji Manufacturing wasn't deterred, and to my surprise, Mr. Miahira dumped Mitsui Trading in order to clear the way for the business venture with me. He went to Nomura Trading and asked them to fill in the role of importing on behalf of Fuji and PACO. Nomura Trading was a major player in all the areas of the international business. In terms of steel trading, Nomura's main market had been Southeast Asia, and they had begun to look to the U.S. market in the 1970s. Mr. Miahira and I visited Nomura's branch office in Los Angeles and met with its manager, Mr. Sasaki.

I liked Mr. Sasaki right away, a warm and genuine person about my age with two children about the same age as my children. We discussed the beam market in general, talking mostly about the difficulties in breaking into the steel beam market. Mr. Sasaki was very familiar with the market condition, and I was impressed with his knowledge. He also knew about my experience at Mark Crest as the Chief Engineer and as one of the top performers in sales from Miahira's briefings. Mr. Sasaki said that he was impressed with my performance, adding, "Because of the nature of the new product, we need a sales engineer. I agree with your approach one hundred percent."

Mr. Sasaki asked to visit my office, and I invited him to my office at home. As he walked into my home, he appeared uncomfortable. He had expected to see a normal office with desks and a bank of telephones glistening under fluorescent lights, not the living room of my home. Sue was instrumental in turning Mr. Sasaki around. Sensing his discomfort, Sue said in her impeccable Japanese, "PACO is not much to look at right now, but Mr. Paik's potential is huge. We pledge our utmost to hold up our end. I firmly believe that you will prosper with PACO by your side."

Mr. Sasaki was impressed with her. I met with him several times more, and from our meetings and through his own independent checking, he recognized my knowledge in the industry and he saw the win-win arrangement for all the parties.

With the 3-way business arrangement in force, I got busy on the marketing plan while we finalized the product design. We met regularly to strategize our plans over tea at fast food restaurants and over family barbecues on weekends. It took Fuji a while before they produced the inventory that we needed. In the meantime, we talked about a stockpile of unsold beams from a failed venture, sitting in Los Angeles harbor as well as San Francisco and Portland. There were about 4,000 tons of beams, valued at $1.2 million, just sitting there.

I suggested that we take over the inventory and move them. Mr. Sasaki thought that it was a great idea and we decided to pursue the project. At first, Mr. Sasaki suggested that I work for a sales commission because I didn't have the money to buy the inventory. I didn't like the arrangement and I said so. I told him that I wanted to take over the inventory on credit and pay them back as I sold it off. He understood what I wanted and he went to work on the Nomura organization to buy the inventory and let me sell them.

In deciding to buy the inventory, Nomura had to consider a number of things because, if the beams didn't sell, Nomura would get stuck with it. They would have to rely on PACO to move the inventory and a big and conservative company like Nomura would never take risks on a green horn like me. PACO was a one-man company, and I was good for no more than $10,000 at that time, and nobody was going to extend me a credit to the tune of $1.2 million. Well, the project looked like it was dead in the water before it got off the ground. However, Mr. Sasaki pursued the idea with Mr. Sukimae at the Nomura headquarters. The two of them discussed the project back and forth and they decided to give it a shot without going through the long, bureaucratic process within Nomura. They told me, "Go ahead and start moving the beams. We will take the responsibility for Nomura."

I was shocked. These two gentlemen were prepared to go out on a limb for me, way out on a limb. They knew about me, but they didn't know me that well. If things went wrong, they could lose their jobs, and they understood that. I understood that they were taking a huge risk, putting their jobs and careers on the line. I was confident about moving the inventory, but they seemed to have more confidence in me than I did.

There was no turning around now. I was committed to make it work. I visited every customer I could think of, but nobody called back. They saw me and talked to me out of courtesy but not to buy. I talked about the advantages and the great pricing until I was blue in the face, but no one was buying. They weren't about to switch their long-time suppliers overnight. It took time to get the green light from any company even if they considered switching suppliers.

I went to Idaho to see a buyer friend at Garden Industry, a mobile home manufacturer. I told him, "I went out on my own. I have some Japanese inventory in Los Angeles. I would like you to buy from me."

My friend hesitated for a long time. He contorted his face like he was in pain and he said finally, "Look, you're my friend, but I can't tell my boss about this Korean guy selling Japanese beams piled up in Los Angeles, San Francisco or Portland. To bring them all the way from West Coast to

Idaho? My boss will think I'm nuts. Sorry, but please understand."

I thought about what he said. He wasn't in the position to give me an order even if he wanted to. I changed tactics. I went to their engineering department and talked with an engineer I knew. While chatting with the engineer about the projects he had on the drawing board, I mentioned about my beams, "I have these beams that will fit your needs." I didn't press him further. I just wanted to sow the seed so to speak and I came home. I knew that he didn't make the final purchasing decision but he had the power to recommend the types of beams, and the purchasing department and the company president went along with the engineer's recommendations. A few days later I called him and asked for his help.

He replied, "Sure. Whatever I can do," and he told the company president and the purchasing manager about my beams and that my beams would work out well. When I called him back he told me what he had done.

I thanked him and presented another idea. I asked him, "How about if I send you some and you try them out. If it works out for you, then, we can talk about buying or not buying."

He liked the idea. He had nothing to lose, everything to gain. He knew that the beams would work out fine. He also knew that my beams would bring down his project cost, and that he would come out a hero if everything worked out. This was an easy idea for him to present to the company president and to the purchasing manager. He said, "As long as I don't have to commit to buying, send them over."

I arranged a truck and sent them a load. They used the beams to fabricate the base frames for some mobile home units, and the beams worked out great without any problems. Everyone at Garden Industry was satisfied with the quality, and the engineer came out looking good because of the improved bottom line. They decided to give me a purchase order, the first one ever for PACO.

chapter 14

CUSTOMER IS KING

With the first purchase order in my pocket, I felt that PACO was the real thing now, not just an idea in my head. I went to another mobile home manufacturer nearby in Idaho and went through the same routine, first, letting them know that I had what they needed and then shipping them the products on a trial basis. The system worked like a champ. Once all the different departments within the company understood the merit of the win-win situation, they came on board. I commuted to Idaho every week almost, talking to the engineers, the buyers and the welders in the plant, giving them pointers and learning from them about the things that made their lives easier. At lunch, I went to the local truck stop to have lunch with truck drivers. I talked to those drivers who carried lumber from Idaho to Los Angeles.

Many of them came back empty from Los Angeles after they unloaded their truck, and I made an arrangement for them to pick up a load of steel rather than returning empty. They were happy to take just $100 for the trouble, which was better than hauling an empty truck. I saved about 50% in transportation by having lunch with the drivers.

In three month's time, I brought in six mobile home manufacturers in Idaho, and the stockpile inventory was gone. Mr. Sasaki at Nomura Trading was impressed. He had been in Los Angeles since 1969 studying the U.S. market and trying to enter the U.S. market without much success. In three months I moved the inventory that no one wanted, and he thought I was hot stuff. The news traveled quickly to Japan, Nomura headquarters and Fuji Manufacturing. They sought to solidify the relationship and expand the operation.

Other Japanese companies heard about the coup as well, and Kawasaki Steel invited me to Japan to talk about a business arrangement with them. They wanted me to represent them in the U.S., and I went there and toured their facilities. I toured Fuji facilities as well and met with the Fuji executives. The Fuji executives gave me a lot of attention, eager to have me join the company. I thanked them for the offer but I declined by saying, "I left a corporation to go on my own.

Now you want me to go back to being an employee." They persisted for me to join Fuji, but I opted for expanding our relationship between Fuji and PACO. Fuji relented in the end, and we concluded my visit by pledging more cooperation between the two companies.

The new business arrangement made PACO the sole distributor in the U.S. for Fuji Manufacturing, and I went to work in developing the market in California while continuing to supply my customers in Idaho. At that time, there was a big company called Silver Crest Mobile Home Manufacturing. I went to see the engineer in charge of the operation, and then the chairman and the founder of the company, Mr. Herman. In a lunch meeting with Mr. Herman, I said, "I did all right as an engineer, but now I want to be a businessman like you. I would like to ask for your help."

He appreciated my candor and he was glad to see me when I visited him a couple times a week. He liked my persistence, too, and he gave me a shot at supplying beams to one of his plants. Once I became a supplier, I stopped by to see him more frequently whether he needed anything or not. I stuck my head in his office. If he was busy, I moved on. If not, we chatted about world affairs, business news, the kids, and schools. After a while it became a daily routine, and the receptionist would joke, "We gotta set up an office for you."

I liked the atmosphere there and I thought it was due to Mr Herman's relaxed style. He would tell me once in a while, "Your beams are too high priced," and smile. He would tell me that half jokingly, and I would reply in mock disdain, "Yeah, yeah, I hear you." Even though he said it in jest, I took it to heart. I lowered his price by one dollar a ton every time a new order came in. It wasn't much of a discount, but it showed that I was listening to him, and he appreciated it. Our relationship began with candor and he didn't see me as a salesman who was out for a quick buck. Rather, he saw me as an honest guy and we enjoyed the open and honest relationship.

I saw him just about every day for several months. Then I began travelling out of town. When I returned from trips I made a point to see him and tell him how things went. He greeted by calling me a "one-man company" or a "suitcase company." I took it as a sign of closeness between the old gentleman and me. Besides, he was right. I was a suitcase company, hauling my suitcase and a briefcase all over the western states and the old guy had me pegged correctly. He was my professor and I was his student, and I enjoyed the classroom, the world of the steel business. I felt fortunate to have him around, and one day, he said, "Young, why don't you start shipping to the rest of the plants?" He said it so casually as though he was asking me to deliver a pizza or something.

My mouth must have dropped a mile. I was speechless for a long time.

He smiled wide and asked, "Did you hear me?"

I nodded, and he laughed.

His huge order was totally unexpected, and my mind raced with numbers, the number of trucks, the number of tons I needed to ship every month, the number of beams in the inventory, and the number of plants he had. I was good with numbers, but these numbers were too big even for me to fathom right then. I finally said, "I gotta sit down and figure this out."

He laughed aloud and said, "You do that."

I raced out of there and got in the car. I needed to go home and check the files and all the data. All the way home, I was thinking, *holy smokes, do I have enough stock inventory to pull this off? It's going to take a lot of trucks. Do I have enough money to pay for the shipping? How many tons do these plants use every month? Wait till Sue hears about this. What's Sasaki going to say?*

Sue wasn't home. She was probably out picking up the kids from school.

I called Sasaki, and he was ecstatic. He couldn't believe the order. He kept asking, "For real? For real?" and I had to calm him down. After the excitement died down, he said he would analyze the inventory sheets and the future shipments from Fuji right away. I got busy figuring out the shipping requirements and the schedule, calling all the plants for the beam sizes and the tonnage they required every month and the delivery dates.

As it turned out, there was enough stock inventory to get by for just two months for the customers in Idaho and now the first customer in California. This was too tight, and Sasaki went to work on extending more credit for PACO from Nomura's end.

Miahira from Fuji was like Sasaki, incredulous and ecstatic. He went to work on the shipping schedule from the factory. We had to move fast and furious to meet the schedule. But this was a nice problem to have, and we worked day and night to make the project work out.

I gave Silver Crest the news that we could manage the order. He nodded nonchalantly and said, "I knew you could do it. Now let's go to lunch."

Thus, the largest deal to date was sealed, and I thanked him profusely.

He replied, "No need to thank me. You are helping me," and patted my shoulder.

I was thankful for the order, yes, but I came away with something more valuable than the order itself. Over the course of our association he taught me about customers, what they wanted and what they needed. It wasn't enough to have the best and the cheapest product on the block. The popular belief around the steel industry then was, "If you have the good products, they'll buy."

That was wrong, I believed. My operation was based on customers. The customer was king and I started with what was in his head, not "how can I sell him my beams." When you sit across from a customer you can pretty much tell what he is thinking, what he feels. I think about what he needs, what he wants, before I think about telling him how wonderful my product is. For example, my customers were always concerned about delivery. It was very crucial that the beams arrived at the customer's plant on time, when they needed them. They didn't want to stockpile on their yards, either. They wanted them as they needed them, and I paid a great deal of attention to their production schedules. I streamlined my delivery schedule to their needs and I always kept the promise date. I worked like a fiend to keep the date, anticipating all the things that could go wrong in shipping tons of steel beams across the western states. Sure, there were traffic problems, accidents, equipment problems and sickness and so on. I had all these contingencies worked out ahead of time, and I regarded these inevitable problems as "excuses" not "justified causes for delay." I hated to call a customer and say, "The delivery is going to be late because..." Because nothing. I knew exactly where all the trucks were all the time and I was never late.

I say again, I was never late.

Customers loved me for my fiendish attitude, and they learned to rely on me and trust me. It was hard work to get to the point of hearing people say, "If Young says so, it must be right." And I achieved that status and the reputation among my customers. So when I told them that I had the lowest price, they believed me. They didn't bother to check other prices. For this reason, I made sure I had the lowest price. I didn't say things like, "I'll match the lowest price in the market." I made sure, instead. My true value was in the customer's trust in me, not the orders I received.

These principles guided me always, and one year to the day of walking into the Garden Industry office in Idaho, PACO's market share jumped to 30% in the light steel industry in the western states. Nobody dreamed of such a tremendous growth for a "one-man, one-suitcase" company, and the Japanese executives marveled, "You did the impossible. PACO is now a real company."

PACO's performance became a main topic among the steel people in Japan as well. They were keenly aware of the market resistance in the U.S. against the Japanese steel, and they couldn't understand how I overcame the resistance while all other steel exporting endeavors showed no sign of life. They wanted to know how I did it and many of them visited us, Sasaki, Miahira and me. I got a kick out of watching Sasaki explain to the visitors, "We set a sales target every month. If we set it at 10,000 tons, he sells 15,000 tons."

chapter 15

SUMITOMO STEEL

How do I explain the American market to the visiting Japanese executives? They were calling me a miracle worker, enticing me to spell things out for them. I told them, "When I was an engineer I focused on the physical aspects, the technology and the ideas. As a businessman, I concentrate on the customer first. Second, customer. Third, customer."

They understood.

Sasaki had a different way of explaining the American market by telling them about playing golf at La Quinta Country Club in Palm Springs, California. He likened the American market to the legendary La Quinta, the exclusive private club that President Eisenhower used to frequent. Dubbed as the "Western White House" during Eisenhower days, it was a famous PGA site that appeared on television often.

Sasaki told the Japanese guests, "PACO-san and I wanted to play there and went there one day. PACO-san approached the golf pro and asked him, 'We're visitors here. Can you let us play here?' The golf pro replied haughtily, 'No visitors. You have to play with a member. If you don't know any member here you can't play.' We lingered around for a while trying to talk the pro into letting us play, but without success. We came out and stood around the entrance pissed off at the way the pro treated us."

"'What the hell's the big deal?' we were saying, and just then a club member was going into the clubhouse. PACO-san grabbed him and asked him, 'We would like to play this golf course but we need a club member to play with. Could you invite us to play with you?' The gentleman looked at us for a while and he said, 'Okay. Meet me here tomorrow morning at ten.'"

Sasaki continued, as our guests were fascinated with the story. "We went there in the morning, not knowing whether the guy would show up or not. If he didn't show up, we were dead in the water. We didn't know his telephone number or anything. We went there hoping that he would be there, and he was there. We played a great round with the gentleman. His house was right on the course, so he even invited us for a beer afterwards. Leaning against the bar at his house, PACO-san said to me, 'Sasaki-san, see? There's nothing impossible.'"

The guests exploded with expletives. "Wahh! Unbelievable!"

Sasaki told them of another instance whereby we were faced with selling tons of hot rolled beams that Kawasaki Kenzai (Kawaken) had made and Nomura had imported. We didn't know why they produced such a competitive item. The market was saturated with the similar prodcuts made by many U.S. companies. Nevertheless, we were faced with the task of selling them and they weren't moving. They tried calling on the distributors around big cities like Los Angeles and San Francisco without much success. Sasaki told me one day, "Let's try the Mao's Red Book method."

I asked him what it was.

He explained that he had to memorize Mao Tse Tung's Red Book cover to cover when he went to China as a representative for Nomura in 1968. That was the requirement back then in order to remain in China and do business there, and he recalled how Mao initiated the revolution in China. Mao wanted to take over the cities, but he didn't start in on the cities right away. He began securing the country-side first, making his way towards the cities gradually. Sasaki asked me, "Why don't we use Mao's strategy and focus on the end users in the countryside first and then go after the big warehouses in big cities?"

It sounded okay to me as far as the strategy went and I began scouring small towns as I made calls to manufacturing shops throughout Idaho and California, giving them favorable terms and conditions, and they started to take on the product. Once the small suppliers and the shops took on the product, the big distributors began taking notice because of the pricing structure and the terms. We managed to clear the inventory and everyone breathed easily.

When we went to Japan, Sasaki repeated the story over there whenever he had a chance, delighting the listeners. Sasaki was a shameless promoter of my abilities to the point of embarrassment, and PACO's star was rising in the land of the rising sun. We were in Japan to solve a technical problem Fuji was having with welded joints. The Fuji beams were constructed in such a way that there were more welded joints than the beams made by other manufacturers. More welded joints meant more potential problems in the customer's shop because of the imperfection near the joints.

This problem caused a lot of headaches in terms of marketing, and Nomura Trading turned its eyes towards Sumitomo Steel.

Sumitomo was one of the largest conglomerates in Japan, and its steelworks was one of the largest in the world. It produced higher quality beams, and Nomura Trading lobbied for the welded beams out of their plant. Sumitomo produced welded beams only for domestic use and it wasn't interested in exporting. Miahira came to the rescue. Before he came to Fuji, he worked at Sumitomo Steel and he knew the major players within Sumitomo. Even though he was a

Fuji employee now, he thought that Sumitomo products were superior to that of Fuji and he made a connection for us to get together with Sumitomo. Miahara persisted and arranged a meeting with Mr. Oya, Sumitomo's manager. At the meeting, Mr. Oya was reluctant about exporting welded beams to the U.S. but he agreed to bring it up to the Sumitomo hierarchy for a discussion. After about three months of discussion, they reached a conclusion that it made sense for Sumitomo to export the welded beams. Sumitomo, Nomura, and PACO entered into a business arrangement, and a new era began for PACO.

chapter 16

CORRUGATED BEAM

PACO's status climbed considerably in the stateside, having joined forces with Sumitomo Steel. Armed with Nomura's expanded financial commitment, PACO was taking shape as a major player. I saw new respect in my customers' eyes as I made my rounds. The humble beginning with the 4,000-ton stockpile in 1975 grew to 50,000-ton annual volume in two years. PACO's future looked brighter than ever. I had focused on seven western states up to that point, and I'd yet to touch the market in the Midwest, the South, and the East.

The Sumitomo hierarchy was very supportive, even so far as to let me change the configuration of the beams for use in Texas. The state of Texas required taller and stronger beams like everything else in the state. I hesitated about changing the design, but the size of the market warranted the complicated procedure. The Sumitomo plant didn't object to the new line because of the huge potential in Texas. Within one year, the new Texan beams took off like crazy, prompting Sumitomo to dispatch a team of commerce type fellows to follow me around wherever I went. The head of business development visited me often as well, practically taking up residence in Los Angeles. They meant to study my operations, and they came to know everything about what I did, how I did it, including the profit margin.

After Texas, calls came in from Georgia and Florida. They just called in the orders, having heard about PACO from their colleagues. This was a pleasant surprise for Sasaki and me, and we cheered about the new market that had showed up at our doorstep without us having to lift a finger.

Our cheering didn't last long, though. Sumitomo stepped in about this time. I got a call from the Director of International Division, who told me, "Stay on this side of Mississippi."

I didn't take too kindly to the idea, needless to say. I protested strongly, "This is different from our original agreement!" and I went on a tirade. But I saw that I wasn't going to do much good over the telephone and I got on the airplane immediately and met with the Sumitomo executives in Japan. I was furious. I tried to change their position, but I was banging my head against a wall.

They replied, "The directive comes from the top management. There's nothing we can do. Sorry." That was the gist of it.

Boy, was I hot. Sumitomo was showing its true colors, I felt. The bastards had this in mind all along. They hooked me just to see how things were going and as soon as things looked rosy and promising, the sons of bitches got greedy all of a sudden. They didn't even want to get into the venture to start with. They hemmed and hawed for three months not knowing what to do, and now they wanted to get in on the act after I did all the groundwork, the design, and the marketing. I challenged them, "I introduced Sumitomo in the U.S. market, and is this what I get?"

The Sumitomo executives said that the situation was out of their hands and asked for my understanding. They repeated that the top management was set on the idea and there was nothing they could do. I took this response as their way of saying f-you, and I was right. They understood the situation all too clearly. Without Sumitomo, I was sunk, and Sumitomo was feeling like they didn't need me any more, confident that they could service the market on their own. They had me. They had the big bucks, and I was just a small fry who had started as a one-man company.

I saw that my argument was futile and got on the plane back home. It was a long trip home as I mulled over the situation and what they had told me. They told me that Sumitomo was only protecting its interest by limiting PACO to the west of Mississippi. They didn't want to depend solely on PACO for the huge market. What if something happened to PACO, what if I died all of a sudden? Sumitomo didn't want to die with PACO, they said, they wanted to limit their exposure. Ha! It was a load of b.s. that they were feeding me. They could worry about their exposure after I died. The truth of the matter was that the market was set for anyone to walk in now and take over. So what if I died today or tomorrow? At this rate they could tell me to get lost all together and there was nothing I could do. They could cut me off any time, and I would have no recourse. What am I going to do? Sue them? Lot of good that was going to do against a giant like Sumitomo. I needed another option. "I can't roll over and play dead now," I thought, "I put in too much sweat and blood into the business. It's my life, and I can't depend on Sumitomo. I can't switch to another supplier, either, because the stake is too big now for anyone to jump in just like that."

I needed another option and I racked my brains to figure it out. What I needed most of all was protection. I needed a legal document that spelled out what was mine—my design, for instance. I thought of applying for a patent for my designs so that Sumitomo wouldn't be able to kick me around so freely.

I went to work on a new patent. I put together several designs and the paperwork for the patent application and sent it in to the patent office. They answered with a note that the existing patents already covered my application and that the application was denied. This happened a few times, and I went after something more unique and different than what I had.

I started all over. I went back to the basics and focused on the idea of making beams stronger and lighter than ever before. The problem was that there was no such thing as "stronger and lighter." Usually, a stronger beam meant a heavier beam, not a lighter one. I wrestled with the idea for a long time to the point of obsession, talking to myself at dinner and in bed. One night I came home and laid down to go to sleep but I couldn't sleep, staring at the ceiling in the dark. Suddenly, a thought came to me and I sat up. I saw a picture in my head, a building or a warehouse made of corrugated metal and I asked myself, "How about the corrugated beam web?" And I saw the evenly spaced wrinkle straight up and down on the web just like the corrugated metal wall.

I ran to the living room. I took a sheet of paper and folded it and opened it out like an accordion and stood it up. It stood on the table stronger than the regular flimsy piece of paper. I held a sheet of regular paper on its edge and saw that it was wobbly without any strength. Then I put my hand on the corrugated paper and it held the weight of my hand. That's it, I said. I looked around for something made of metal. I ran to the kitchen and took a can of Coca Cola out of the refrigerator. I poured out the liquid and opened up the can with scissors and laid it flat on the table. On the flat sheet of aluminum I drew a series of parallel lines with a ball pen and a straight edge. The lines got dented a little bit, which made the sheet of aluminum look like a miniature corrugated wall and I shook it. It was no longer flimsy like a sheet of aluminum but sturdy and stiff. I held the corrugated aluminum sheet on its edge with the lines going up and down. I put pressure on the top edge, and the sheet held its

THE DO OR DIE ENTREPRENEUR

shape strong and steady. I became excited. The effect was much better on the aluminum than it was on the paper. Next step was to try the same kind of accordion wrinkles on a steel sheet.

I'd have to wait until the morning to test the concept on steel and I lay down to go to sleep. I couldn't sleep. My head was filled with crimping steel plates, setting up the hydraulic press to indent straight lines up and down on a web plate, and I waited up for day break. At dawn I raced down to the office and set up a thin steel plate, the same one from the beam, and made a series of dents straight up and down. Sure enough, the web plate yielded twice the strength over the plain one. I ran the numbers and the numbers worked out so that I could cut down the weight 25 to 30 percent. In terms of production cost, I could cut down 20 to 30 percent.

"This is it!" I yelled for joy, and made up more models and tested them over and over. It took me half a year to come up with the new idea since Sumitomo had let me down. I called my patent attorney and began the patent process. He made the patent application, and we waited. Six months later the patent attorney called. He said cheerfully, "The application looks like it's going to make it. You'll get it by the end of 1979."

I was excited. "Oh, man, finally. I got my own patent."

I called Sumitomo and told them, "I developed a new beam. I'll bring the prototype and we can talk about it."

I got on the plane to Japan. I met with Mr. Takahashi who was in charge of engineering and explained everything. Then I proposed for Sumitomo to produce the beam and sell them.

Mr. Takahashi said, "Let's study it and decide."

I agreed and came back home.

Sumitomo took forever to study the corrugated beam. The engineering team dragged their collective tails and talked about the theories instead of testing the corrugated beam. They couldn't find the way to calculate the strength because they didn't know how to do it. They had never seen anything like that before. Some of them went as far as saying that they didn't see it in any textbooks, so it was a fake.

Hearing this, I became angry. I countered strongly, "Look, who do you think made textbooks and all the theories in them? They're made by humans, not God. If a new technology comes out, you change the textbook, not the other way around. How can you call it a fake?"

They gave me more mumbo jumbo and I decided to

demonstrate the concept to the Sumitomo engineers. I asked Mr. Takahashi to call a meeting for his engineering department and I flew to Japan. At the meeting, I stayed away from talking about theories. Instead, I pulled out an empty Coca Cola can. I opened it up and made a series of lines with a ball pen and a straight edge. Then I took the corrugated can and shook it in front of them, and they saw how sturdy it was.

They thought it was interesting then. Most of them nodded, but some of them expressed doubt because it was too simple and elemental.

I countered, "If it's too simple, why didn't you think of it all these years? It may not be a grand invention, but it is very effective."

One engineer pulled out of the meeting quietly then. I learned later that he went to the testing room. He took a beam and pressed a series of dents into the web and reported the test results to the meeting that the same beam turned two, three times stronger. Mr. Takahashi and the other engineers were convinced then.

I told Mr. Takahashi that I had applied for the patent and that the patent is almost ready. Then I said, "If Sumitomo isn't interested in producing the corrugated beam, I'm going to find another steel beam manufacturer."

He understood where I was coming from. He told his superiors about my position, and the ball started rolling. The same day, the president of Sumitomo asked Mr. Takahashi to take a serious look at the corrugated beam.

I received the patent from the U.S. Patent Office on January 2, 1980. Shortly after, Sumitomo and I entered into an agreement to manufacture the corrugated beam, with PACO as the sole distributor for the U.S.

chapter 17

TRIALS AND TRIBULATIONS

The news of the corrugated beam hit the industry like a tornado. "Newsweek" magazine reported it first in the "New Technology" section, followed by other trade magazines and newspapers across the country. Foreign newspapers picked it up, too. The Japanese press, especially, went nuts over the news. I got letters from all over the world, even from the Soviet Union, requesting more detailed information about the corrugated beam. I counted over 1,000 letters.

PACO customers were excited about the corrugated beam and they wanted me to explain the new technology. I always carried a supply of Coca Cola cans with me and I used them to explain the improved strength just as I had explained to the Japanese engineers. My customers went wild over it. They couldn't wait until the new beams arrived in the U.S.

The favorable reception made me feel great. I was on top of the world with all the attention by the media. Everyone was happy for me, making a big fuss over the corrugated beam wherever I went. I thought I had it made now and I decided to concentrate on the corrugated beam, where the big money was.

I told Sumitomo Steel, "I'm going to concentrate on the new beams. Let someone else handle the regular welded beams."

Once the new beams arrived, I went to see my customers. I walked into their offices thinking that they would give me the orders just for the asking. I said, "The new beams are here now. I'm going to handle the new ones only from now on. So don't use the old ones any more. Switch over to the new ones."

I was wrong to think that the customers would line up to take shipments of the new beams. The customers replied initially, "The beams look great, but let us give it some thought." When I followed up, they responded, "I want to see how other guys do with it before I start using them."

I was stunned by the reluctance. These were my loyal customers, and no one was willing to make a move on the lighter and stronger beams. I didn't understand what was going on. I had washed my hands off the regular welded beams and piled up a huge inventory of corrugated beams, thinking that I would have my handful. But my customers wanted to stay with the regular beams.

After a couple of months the situation didn't change. I went to the largest customer and set up a testing session in his factory. I sought to gain his approval, figuring that the smaller companies would follow his lead. I let everyone know what was happening with the testing. The word got around, and my competitors got the wind of it as well. My competitors joined forces to sabotage the testing, even as to slip a few bucks to the tester under the table to produce negative results. The test was a flop.

The storm was gathering around PACO's new corrugated beam, the b.s., the vicious rumors, and innuendoes with it. I wasn't ready for any of this. My modus operandi was based on honesty and trust all along, which led to my success, the only way I knew how to be. And here I was, being bombarded with lies, and I had no idea how to deal with them.

My customers told me, "Hey, Young, I hear your beam's too thin. Blows holes when you try to weld on'em."

Blood rushed to my head when I heard things like that. I

shouted, "What? Who the hell told you that? It's lie, a damn lie!" I argued and tried to set them straight, but the damage was done. There was no turning the customer around.

There wasn't much I could do other than going back to my office with my head down. At the office, I dreaded the sound of the telephone ring. I jumped whenever it rang for fear that it bore bad news like, "We tested your new beams, and we can't use them. Come and get your test beams out of here." What used to be the most welcome sound just a year before turned ugly for me, the sound I had associated with the sound of the cash register.

The company till was empty, paying for the warehouse with the useless corrugated beams piled up high and wide, and I was sick. I was sick to think that I had failed, a failure as a businessman, a father, and a husband. I regretted having ventured into the business world, wishing that I had stayed on as an engineer in comfort.

Two years into the most painful period of my life, tougher to endure than the days as a war refugee, I became physically weak. Come New Years Day in 1983, I decided that I could not go on like this. I needed to change my life and recover my strength. I started to swim every day. I was up at 4:30 every morning and I swam countless laps, trying to clear my mind and focusing on rebuilding my strength. The water was good, taking me back to the day in Busan, when my uncle gave me money for a long bath. I recalled how exhilarating the bath was, the first one in three months after the arduous journey south not knowing if I was going to die from bullets or starvation. My mind and body suspended alone in the big pool took me back to the days when death was as common as the hamburger, and I wept. I wept for my mother and my father and my brother and the little ones. Then the small lake I used to swim in as a child in Chestnut Grove. Then outside Van Wert, Ohio, when I took Sue to swim in the water pond in the old rock quarry. Yes, that was a warm, sunny day when I pushed Sue into the pond playfully only to find that she couldn't swim. It never occurred to me that she couldn't swim. How could anyone not swim? I had to jump into the water and pull her out of there. Poor Sue. What was I thinking? Oh, my God, what was I thinking? Then my three children splashing and laughing.

As days wore on I swam more laps, feeling less tired. It was in that pool of lives that I decided to start all over again. No, I wasn't going to die like this, not after I beat death so many times during the war and afterwards. I didn't come this far to die like this. I still had much to do. I had to find my brother.

I crawled back to Sumitomo. I asked them to let me sell the regular beams as well as the corrugated beams. After much groveling and pleading, they gave me back my sales territory, west of Mississippi. Talk about eating crow, I became a humble man again.

I began knocking on doors all over again with a changed attitude and the three principles in selling. That is, first, the customer, second, the customer, and the third, the customer. I became the "one-man, one-suitcase company" all over again, the original PACO man from ten years before, focusing on what the customer wanted, not what I thought they needed.

chapter 18

THE ROAD BACK

Customers appreciated the fact that I was offering them options, the regular beam and the corrugated beam. They told me what they wanted, and I listened. I marketed the regular beams like the old days, and I offered the corrugated beams on a trial basis. Engineers were more receptive to the new beams and they accepted the idea of trying them out without any commitment to buy. In terms of testing, I hired a number of testing companies spread out all over, rather than relying on one tester.

Slowly, the customers tried using the corrugated beams and acknowledged the superior performance in terms of the overall profitability. The vicious rumors faded one by one, and I felt better about the beam's future.

The big break came when FAB TECH decided to use the

corrugated beam. I had asked an engineer at FAB TECH to try out the beams a while back, and he called me. I took the call and I recognized him, an engineer who had graduated from Georgia Tech about the same time I graduated Indiana Tech. He was a fine man, and we swapped college stories. He said, "The corrugated beam is okay. I'm trying to cut down the project cost by using this beam. Can you give me a good price?"

I replied, "Of course. Whatever you want the price to be." Thus, FAB TECH became the first customer for the corrugated beams.

Then Fleetwood began taking shipments, a few hundred tons at a time, and the word got around to other customers, who in turn showed more interest because of Fleetwood's status as one of the leaders in the industry. The engineers from other big companies began calling me, saying, "I want to take another look at it." They were attracted to the pricing structure that made Fleetwood products far more competitive than their own.

This was the break I needed, long overdue. Then the president of Fleetwood, Grand Kummer and the chairman of the Board, John Crean called me directly and said, "We are producing new RV's. We want to use the corrugated beams to reduce the weight for the new RV line. Is it possible to change the beam design a little?"

I knew exactly what he had in mind. He wanted to make the RV lighter to improve the fuel economy. I jumped at the chance. "Not only the design change, but I'll get you whatever you need." I was on the airplane to Georgia immediately. Fleetwood engineers and I worked out all the details and wrote out a contract. The president issued a directive to all the plants, "From now on, use corrugated beams for all locations."

That little statement was my savior, my Messiah, and I looked to the sky and said a prayer of thanks.

Sue cried. She had been the rock, the steady force that held everything together, and she shed happy tears, "I knew it, I knew you could do it."

chapter 19

NEGOTIATING FOR LTV

By the time the corrugated beams started moving steadily, the business activity for the regular beams recovered to where I had left it. It took a full year for the business to turn around from the time I began rebuilding. I stuck to the customer-first-second-third policy with religious fervor, flying across the country like a man possessed. I concentrated on Fleetwood of Georgia, the main customer for the corrugated beam, and the surrounding area. A permanent fixture on short flights in Georgia, Florida, and the Carolina's, I became friends with flight attendants and the folks at the ticket counter. I saw my customers on these flights often and I always flew economy class whether I was going to Atlanta, Macon, Savannah, Tampa or Charleston. I wouldn't be caught dead in the first class cabin even though the seats were more comfortable there, especially on long flights. I didn't want to take a chance on my customers seeing me fly first class, leading them to think that I was getting fat on their hard-earned money.

Even though the business was growing steadily, I wanted to make sure that the customers knew that they were getting the best price from me, and my respect. The competitors continued to feed rumors like, "It's companies like PACO that make it hard on domestic steel manufacturers by importing Japanese steel." I couldn't afford a perception that I was harming the domestic steel industry by what I was doing. Nothing could be further from the truth. It was never my intention to cause the decline in the domestic steel industry. I only looked to servicing my customers as best as I could, and they rewarded me by giving me orders.

Nevertheless, I was very sensitive to what my competitors were saying, and I wasn't about to give them any excuse to spread more rumors. In fact, I sought to do business with Chaparral Steel, a domestic producer of wide flange beams from Texas. Chaparral Steel came on the scene in 1982 as a brand new steel mill and it began producing Panthom beams in earnest in 1984 in order to compete against the welded beams. Outfitted with new equipment and new technology, Chaparral stormed the market with the slogan, "lowest priced steel products in the world." Also, in announcing their entrance into the welded beam market, they made it very plain that they were going after the imported beams.

Naturally, I was very interested in carrying their product line and I approached them a number of times, but they refused to sell to PACO. They saw me as one of the bad guys. As far as they were concerned, I was instrumental in bringing in the imported beams, rocking the boat in the domestic steel industry. I saw how they could feel that way. After all, I did have a 30 percent market share in the light-weight steel beams by way of Sumitomo products. But I didn't think much of their anti-import position. I felt that they were waving a flag, touting a form of protectionism. Protectionism has no place in the free market system, be it in the U.S. or in Japan. Customers want the best service, the best product, and the best price for their money, and in the end, the customers determine the marketplace.

Regardless of my business philosophy, I found myself on the other side of the fence as far as Chaparral was concerned, and we squared off against each other. Chaparral's aggressiveness took hold in Texas because of its proximity, taking away many of my customers. I lowered my price many times to stay ahead of Chaparral, but they came right back with lower prices, and maintained their dominance in the Texas market. They pushed hard in other regions as well, but PACO managed to maintain the annual volume of 50,000 to 80,000 tons, owing to the competitiveness of the lighter corrugated beams.

At times, I ran out of inventory because of Sumitomo's limited capability of 50,000 tons per year. I supplemented the inventory with Chaparral products that I bought through the back door using a good customer of mine. The inventory shortage problem came up more often than I liked. I hated to tell a customer that I didn't have the beams to sell him.

The problem persisted, and I looked to the European mills for help. I went to Europe to arrange for hot rolled beams with ABE Steel of Luxembourg. ABE products did well, its volume growing steadily. People were already familiar with the hot rolled beams that were similar to the domestic products, and I didn't have to go through the pain of introducing a new concept like the welded beam and the corrugated beam.

Some people raised their eyebrows, "How come PACO only sells imported beams, first the Japanese and now European?"

I countered the charge with, "I would handle the domestic beams if Chaparral sold them to me."

I continued to wear the anti-domestic image uncomfortably. When the president of LTV called me one day, I had in mind to buy supplies from the huge steel company, second only to U.S. Steel. Unexpectedly, LTV's president, David Hoag, asked me if I could come to Salt Lake City, Utah. Although he was a young man in his forties, he was considered an icon in the steel industry, heading up the public company with steel mills in Pittsburgh, Chicago, Cleveland and Dallas. He wouldn't say what he wanted to see me about, but I accepted his invitation nevertheless.

Sitting down with him and his assistants at dinner, he asked me, "You didn't come all the way here just to have dinner with me. Did you meet your customers here?"

I told him that I had arranged several meetings with my clients in Salt Lake City and finished my business with them.

He said, "I admire that. You're a hard worker. That's why you're doing so well. I think it's tough for my salesmen to stay up with you." I thanked him and I asked him what he wanted to talk about. He mentioned that he was exploring the ways to help each other. He asked me, "I would like to invite you to our Pittsburgh office. Will that be all right?"

I replied, "Whenever you want."

After dinner he asked me, "What is your wish?"

I replied honestly, "I want to run a big steel company like you."

He was surprised at my answer and he exclaimed, "No problem!" He showered me with accolades, saying that I was all of what he had expected to see.

I felt flattered by his recognition, the unfettered attention from a steel industry icon, and my chest ballooned up with pride. I had truly arrived.

Two weeks later I went to Pittsburgh like I had promised. I walked into David Hoag's office and saw several of his staff along with an attorney.

I sat down, and he started by saying, "Instead of competing with you, we want to cooperate with you. We would like you to handle all our lightweight beam market. What do you think?"

I didn't understand what he was getting at right away and I hesitated at first, but I understood that he wanted me to come in as the president in charge of the Junior beam operation for LTV.

Actually, LTV was on shaky grounds at the time despite its huge scale. Pittsburgh had been the center of the steel industry for 30 years after World War II, producing more than half of the global output. Slow to modernize the plants, the American steel industry was losing ground to the newer facilities in Japan and Korea. LTV was no exception, and it was looking to streamline the operations, trying to minimize the losses and stop the bleeding. I sympathized with David Hoag and his effort to salvage as much as he could in a hostile climate in which the shareholders clamored for profit and dividend checks on one hand, while the newspapers reported the long unemployment lines around Pittsburgh.

I knew what everyone else knew in the steel industry: LTV needed a massive capital infusion to modernize its plants. Instead, it was focusing on reorganization, chopping away the unprofitable divisions to satisfy the belligerent investors and the shareholders, whose motivation was profit, not more debt. The situation was hopeless, and I knew it. David Hoag was just prolonging the agony, and I knew that, too.

I replied, "I can't do that. It's tough to leave what I'm doing." And I told him that my ambition lay in running my own company, not for someone else even if it was for LTV. He kept at me, making me incredible offers. I thanked him repeatedly for the honor, the consideration given to me as a successor for the Junior beam division. But I declined, saying, "I know what you have in mind. Why don't we look for ways to help each other?" as it was not in my interest to sever the relationship with a giant like LTV.

He asked me at the end, "Are you saying that you want to run the whole company?"

I replied as clearly as I could, "That's correct. But I want to run my own company. I have no desire to run a company for someone else."

About a year after my conversation with David Hoag, I read in the newspapers that LTV had filed for Chapter 11. I wasn't surprised, but the news came as a shock in the States and around the world. A few months later, David Hoag called and asked me to come to his Pittsburgh office.

I met him at his office. He said, "We could ask you to take over the entire rolled section division, but how about buying the company instead?"

I replied, "You know that I don't have that kind of money."

"There are ways to take care of that. But first tell me if you have any inclination."

"As for me, if I could buy it, I couldn't wish for anything else. But I don't have that kind of horsepower. That's the problem."

"You're close to the Japanese company. How about if you team up with them? If not, we can buy it together ourselves."

I asked him about buying it ourselves, and he said for me to invest what I could and guarantee them what I thought was reasonable. He said further that I could call it PACO or LTV. "Once you take over and set up the operation, I'll get the banks to come up with the operating cash."

I thought about the two options. The first option was simpler if I could get Sumitomo to go in on the deal. The second option was complicated because of the endless paperwork that was required by the courts and the length of time that would have taken to process them. I called Sumitomo and floated the idea. "I think we can get it at a good price. Let's buy it together."

Sumitomo wasn't enthused at first. But they didn't kill the idea entirely. They suggested a comprehensive study of LTV before making the final decision. I agreed, and Sumitomo dispatched a study team to Pittsburgh headed up by Mr. Moruoka, the president of the Overseas Operations Division himself. The Pittsburgh newspapers had a field day about all the Sumitomo executives coming and going. One of the papers even printed a report that a Korean named Young

Paik was coming to Pittsburgh to buy LTV and rescue it for all those who lost their jobs.

Of course, that was premature, and it became a nuisance for me to go outside with all the reporters following around, even the reporters from Korea, and all the attention wasn't worth the trouble. I just wanted to get the project moving, and after a month or so of all the preliminary studies, Sumitomo said that they were in. We began talking hard numbers now, the purchase price, the appraised figures for the inventory, the facilities, and all the associated assets. We came up with the number finally and then we moved on to figuring out who was good for how many shares.

I was slated for the CEO's slot so I maintained my position as the major stockholder followed by more than five Japanese companies including Sumitomo Steel, Mitsui Trading and Nomura Trading. When all the dust settled finally, I ended up with around a 30 percent share and the Japanese companies went for between 10 to 15 percent share each.

Then we tackled the staffing, which took a long time to sort out which employees stayed on and who went, and the Japanese contingents made such an ordeal out of it that I just went along with whatever they wanted. I was quick on my feet, but I was alone, while the others loaded up their teams with experts, the accountants and the attorneys, and I didn't have the energy to argue with them.

Finally, all the t's were crossed and the i's dotted, and we set the date and time for the announcement. The day before the scheduled announcement, an instruction came from Japan to hold off on the public announcement until the EPA of the federal government cleared the transaction. We hired a legal expert in environmental law to secure the clearance from EPA. We had daily meetings on the subject for about a month, and I finally gave up despite the Governor's promise to take care of the clearance with the federal government. I called Sue at home and told her, "I'm too tired to continue. I'm coming home to rest for now."

Well, the clearance from EPA never materialized, and it was the deal breaker as it turned out. The process took one year from the beginning to the end, not to mention the money and the sweat that went into the effort, and I was disappointed that Sumitomo had pulled out. What a fiasco that was, and I tried to put it behind me as quickly as possible. Eventually, LTV was picked over by the vultures, and it disappeared from the scene. I felt bad for those LTV employees who devoted their lives to the company. Like

David Hoag, I was confident that I could have made it work, had the deal gone through. All the talking did one thing for me, though. It got me to start thinking about a steel plant of my own.

chapter 20

MOTHER

At home and rested, I went back to my business at hand, concentrating on selling welded beams from Sumitomo, the corrugated beams, and the hot rolled beams from ABE Steel of Luxembourg. I looked in on my customers and I went back to having lunches with truck drivers at truck stops.

Come 1988, the raw metal scrap price jumped up suddenly, and this changed the course of my relationship with another major player in the industry, Chaparral Steel. The hike in raw metal scrap price hit the mills hard all over the country, including Chaparral, prompting them to review their position with respect to PACO, and all the bloody noses we had caused for each other. Chaparral called me unexpectedly, asking for a meeting.

Remembering the long ordeal that David Hoag of LTV and

I had gone through the year before, I wondered what Chaparral had in store for me. They wanted to put an end to our hostile relationship. This was tremendous news, and I almost fell out of my chair. We started talking in earnest, and they told me how they knew about my purchases of Chaparral products through the back door for the past year or so. They wanted me to distribute their products up front instead, and I welcomed the arrangement with open arms. It was a win-win situation for both of us because Chaparral increased their sales volume through PACO, while PACO was able to maintain the inventory without scrambling around.

Also, I didn't have to worry about Chaparral and what they were up to and vice versa. Above all, we would save a lot of time, the time we couldn't afford to waste in trying to outdo each other. They saw the wisdom in joining forces to battle the jump in the scrap and billet price. The production cost jumped, but the customers weren't willing to share the burden. Their sympathy went only so far, and they resisted any price increase. Their attitude was, "What's the billet price got to do with me?" and the suppliers like Chaparral and PACO had to look inward to deal with the crisis.

PACO was no longer a company that sold only the imported beams, and I liked that, too. My customers grumbled less about "that Korean guy who sells Japanese beams." Complaints decreased, too. When they found slag inclusion and undercutting in the welds they had made themselves, they blamed me and the Japanese beam, rather than examining their own welding technique in the shop. I would tell them, "Check the welding rods. Check the amperage. Slag? Yor're running it too hot. You're burning the mother material."

When the welds splattered they blamed the inferior steel quality from Japan. I would explain to them that steel composition was the same, the real iron ore, the same coke, the same process, same everything. The chemical elements didn't change from here to there, I would tell them. They were running the welding machine too hot most likely, but it was easier to blame the steel.(Frankly, domestic steel used scrap metal, resulting in a wrong chemical combination.)

With Chaparral products, I didn't have to explain too much. I handled the complaints by saying, "Hey, this is standard. What are you complaining for?" I didn't have to exchange the rusty beams for them, either. They cleaned the rust off the beams on their own by brushing or grit blasting, and they didn't bug me with it. I have had to exchange Sumitomo beams now and then. Freighted in by ocean, the salty ocean air and the long haul left a coat of rust on the beams, some more than the other, and the customers complained sometimes. I didn't say anything in those incidences. I just sent them new, black beams and had the driver pick up the rusty ones. I had no problems with the customers' complaints. It was their right to complain, and they were always right in my book.

With Chaparral in my corner, life was easier, and for the first time in a long time, I enjoyed watching the company grow steadily without worrying about my backside. There had been too many roller coaster rides up to now, and I felt like I deserved the peace and quiet. Stability is something every businessman craves, and I was no different.

I had everything—a wonderful wife, three nice children, a home in Palos Verdes overlooking the Pacific Ocean, and 60 percent market share in the lightweight steel beam industry. I couldn't ask for more out of my life here in America, especially for a person who had landed with fifty dollars in the pocket and no English. With more time to spend, I ate dinner at home more frequently, even relaxing in the family room with Sue and the children once in a while. At a first glance, we were the picture-perfect family. We'd come a long way, Sue and I. But that wasn't the complete picture.

Deep in my heart I always felt a sense of longing through-out my journey up to this point, my pursuit for education, success, and financial stability for my family. But I never for-got about my family in North Korea, my mother, my broth-ers, and sisters. Good times or bad, they were with me all along, and the more comfortable I became, the more I missed my family. My children, bless their hearts, got the brunt of my angst about my family in North Korea. I would tell them about their grandfather, grandmother, their uncles, and their aunts incessantly. Having been born in America, they had no use for "ancient" history that had occurred far away from their own Southern Californian surroundings.

But Sue sympathized with me. She knew what I was going through, and she and I talked about our lives in the old country like it was yesterday. One day I read an article about an organization that made arrangements to visit the family members in North Korea. I bolted up on my chair and I called them right away and arranged a meeting with Reverend Hong from the group.

I asked the minister whether it was possible for them to arrange a trip for me. He gave me a rundown on how the process worked. "First, we send in your name, birthday, the place of birth, the schools you attended, names of your family members, their age, their address, and so on to Pyongyang."

"Pyongyang!" I mouthed the word as a matter of automatic gesture, the word I had not heard for many years, but I didn't sound it. I let Reverend Hong continue.

He said, "Then after two weeks, we get a reply from them."

"That quickly?" I asked, incredulous that he spoke of the city as though it was a nearby town. Suddenly Pyongyang seemed so close. I felt disoriented, for I had kept Pyongyang in the far corner of my mind, a faraway place I had left forty years before.

Reverend Hong continued, "They'll locate your family and let us know."

I quickly filled out all the information they required and left. I came home and told Sue what I had done. She was excited. At dinner, I began talking about my mother, my brothers and my sisters, my hometown, my father and his anti-communism activities, the war, my escape south, and my life as a refugee. This was the same story I had told my children repeatedly over the years. My children were tired of hearing the story for the hundredth time or more, but I wanted them to remember everything, every detail, so that they would know about their grandmother, uncles and aunts and recognize them when or if they got a chance to meet them someday after I was gone. Subconsciously, I was preparing them to carry on my quest, my duties as the oldest son in the family.

The way the political situation looked in Korean Peninsula over the years, there wasn't much hope that I would see my mother again. But now Reverend Hong's group brought on a breath of hope in me, and I was excited.

Two weeks went by, and no word came from Pyongyang. I waited another week, and still no word. I called the organizers only to hear that there was no news and I waited some more. Three months went by. I guessed that there was a problem because of my father's anti-communism activities, which in turn labeled the family as traitors.

The organizers called and asked to see me one day. At the meeting, I asked them if they had located my family. They didn't say anything. They turned their eyes away from me as though they knew something but they didn't have a heart to tell me.

I knew for sure then that my family was labeled as traitors. I told the group everything about my family. I told them that my father was a supporter of Ahn Chang Ho and

Cho Man Shik, the democratic leaders. He hated the Reds and he worked furiously against the Labor Party and the communists. He was executed for his actions, and as far as North Korea was concerned he and his family were enemies of the state, I told them. I knew all this, I told them, but that was forty years ago. All I wanted now was to find out if my mother was alive, and to see her. I pleaded with them to help me. "You are my only hope," I said.

After the long pleading, they nodded in silence. Now they understood why there was no news from Pyongyang regarding my family. They seemed relaxed now. Pyongyang's silence was not due to a mishap in their line of communication with Pyongyang but my family history.

I said, "My life is in your hands."

The organizers said that they understood the situation and that they would do their best to get me over there.

They went to bat for me. I didn't know what was said and how, but they made it work. Some time later, I received the word that my visit was possible. It was a miracle.

I flew to Japan. From there I flew on China Airline to Beijing. In Beijing I went to the American Embassy and told them about my plan to enter North Korea. I did this at the advice of a fellow traveler, an American banker in Beijing, whom I met on the airplane. We chatted together like old friends on the empty airplane, empty because of the Tianamin Square incident just a few weeks before.

After the American Embassy, the Beijing branch manager of Nomura drove me through the streets that were studded with armed soldiers to the North Korean Embassy. I went there to apply for the entry visa per the instructions given to me by the organizers in Los Angeles. (There is no North Korean Embassy in the U.S.)

Entering the Embassy, my heart skipped a beat or two, recalling the newspaper accounts about kidnappings by North Korean agents, the assassination attempts, and the Rangoon bombing in 1983. I needn't have worried as it turned out. North Korean agents were nowhere in sight. Instead the Consulate General of North Korea greeted me with a smile, saying that he was expecting me. He put me at ease right away, and I relaxed, drinking tea while they prepared my visa. The whole process took only half of an hour, and I was all set with the paperwork.

That afternoon the Embassy staff guided me onto the airplane to Pyongyang. The airplane was filled with men who wore the Kim Il Sung badge on the lapel. I sat next to an

Indian consulate who spoke English. Once I boarded the plane and sat down, I thought of nothing else but my mother and my brother Young-ik, their images dashing about in front of me. My last meeting with Young-ik kept coming into my head. He had run after me in his bare feet up the frozen hill. I could still hear him say, "*Hyung*, older brother, I'm here." He wanted to come with me. He saw me running and he wanted me to take him with me. And I told my kid brother to go back down to the house and look after mother and the little ones. He said, okay, under his breath and turned around with his head down...

His last word and the last image haunted me through the years, those moments I wished I could take back. Maybe now, maybe now. I would hold him tight in my arms and ask for his forgiveness. I would never let him go, I would never let him go, for I shouldn't have let him go then even though the bullets ricocheted all around us.

Now the airplane droned over the Yalu River, drowning out the sounds of guns in Sungchun Valley, once peaceful Chestnut Grove from forty years before. I pressed my face to the small window, looking and looking for the signs of my peaceful past, the lazy pasture where I used to take the orange ox. I had left my childhood down there somewhere, among the chestnut trees, where I used to lie down and stare at the sky endlessly and count the cotton clouds floating by.

I was floating high in the sky now from a different vantage point but just as mystified now as I was then about the world up here and down there. I wondered why I had to fly from Japan to Beijing, crossing the sky over the southern half of the peninsula, then back to the northern half of the same peninsula from Beijing. The heart of Seoul lay 140 air miles away from the heart of Pyongyang, and the zig-zag route made very little sense to a person like me, who had devoted half of his life to efficiency. If I travel from New York to Washington D.C., I would never go west to Detroit first and then back east to Washington D.C. That's asinine and a waste of time and money as far as I am concerned. But that's about what I did by going to Beijing first to get to Pyongyang. But I didn't dwell on the economy of my trip too long. I would have gone to the moon and back to see my mother and my brother.

The plane touched down on Pyongyang airport. I must have straightened my necktie hundred times at least while the plane taxied to the terminal. It didn't take long for the airplane to get to the terminal because it was the only airplane in sight. A guide found me and told me that my sister and my father's sister were waiting for me. I saw the two women in the distance, and I recognized my aunt right away. I ran to her and hugged her. I didn't recognize my sister at all. I was crying with my aunt in my arms and my sister called my name in a way she used to call me with her accent. I recognized the voice, my sister's voice from way back when, and I pulled her into my arms.

In between sobs I asked her, "How's mother?" "She is fine," she said. I asked hurriedly, "And Young-ik?" My sister cried louder and said, "He's gone to the other world."

Too late, I got here too late, I was thinking, and no more words came out from either of us. Clutched together, we went back forty years, crying a tear for each and every day we were apart. For the moment of an eternity, there was no Pyongyang, no Seoul, no North, no South, no sun, no moon, just us, my sister and I, and my aunt too.

I didn't know how long we were frozen in time, until the guide came up to us and said, "I'm sorry but you'll have to part for now and I'll bring you back together in a few days."

Numb and disoriented, I stepped back and looked at the guide like he was an intruder. He was truly apologetic with his eyes cast down, and I realized that I wasn't in my own world. I recalled that I was to undergo an orientation course for two days and I sighed. Two days of orientation and then the meeting with mother. That's how the system worked, and I had no say in the matter.

For two days the guides took me around Pyongyang, visiting Kim Il Sung's statue and Kim Il Sung exhibits. The city was much like Seoul with wide boulevards and tall buildings, except it was much quieter and serene, even beautiful. It was nothing like the place that I saw last, the crumbled city in rubbles and the sounds of explosion all around.

On June 21, 1989, the guides picked me up in a Mercedes Benz and drove me to a village called Anheung Li in Taechon County. I was expecting to go to Sungchun, but mother had moved to the new village about 100 miles north of Pyongyang.

Mother was waiting when I arrived in the village, and there was no mistake in recognizing her even though ninety years of hard life was all too evident in her drawn face and the frail stoop.

"Mother!" That's all I said, that's all I could say. I ran to her and hugged her. She was real, her warmth, her touch, and forty years of absence shrank to nothing. I was a child again, not a father, not a millionaire from America, just a son happy to see his long lost mother.

chapter 21

PYONGYANG—DIFFERENT PLACE, DIFFERENT TIME

When I came home to Palos Verdes, my American family noticed that I was a changed man. Sue and the children marveled at how calm and relaxed I seemed compared to my constant preaching through the years about how things were in the old days, in the old country. The fanaticism was gone from my voice as I told them about the trip to my mother's home, the dreamlike days far, far away from Palos Verdes Peninsula. I told Sue what mother had said, "I thought I had lost all three sons. But here you are, the son I never told anyone about. Heaven sent you to me, and now I can die in peace."

After two days and three nights with my mother, I actually felt grateful that the North Korean powers-to-be had spared her life, and that the short visit was granted to me. I was made to feel privileged to receive this gift of life, and when she told me that I should thank Kim Il Sung the Great Leader for looking after her all these years, I assented. I felt uneasy though, that she would make this request. I wasn't sure that she meant for me to pursue an audience with Kim Il Sung—she had to know how impossible that was—or she was asking me for the local officials to hear. She said this repeatedly, and I thought that she really meant it at times. She didn't say much else with equal conviction, and I felt that something was amiss.

I also found it strange that my mother didn't cry, not one drop of tear, even when we said good-bye not knowing when we would see each other again. She said merely, "I am so happy that heaven sent my son to me. I am very proud of your achievements. My only wish is that you devote yourself to the fatherland and Kim Il Sung the Great Leader. That is the way for you to help the family and me." She said this in front of all the local dignitaries who turned up for my departure.

I said, "Mother, please stay healthy."

Lastly, she asked me to arrange for my nephew to attend a school in Pyongyang, a task I would take on gladly and do whatever else I could do. I shook hands with twenty or so officials, asking them to look after my mother and the family.

Just as the car was ready to take off, three nephews came running to the car, crying and calling me, *"Keun abuji,"* "big father" in straight translation, meaning big uncle. I reminded them of their own missing father, dead and gone as far as we all knew. I hated to leave the children of my brother in the teary state, all the tears they'd been harboring for their father. I held them and cried for their tender hearts, recalling the loss of my own father. I wished to spend time with them, but my limited schedule took me back to Pyongyang.

In Pyongyang, my brother's wife and I went around the city and bought gifts for mother and the family. The department stores were not well-stocked but there was enough clothing, furniture and foodstuff for everyone back in the countryside. The authorities had set mother up with a refrigerator, a television and some furniture with the money I had given to them upon my entrance into the country, but mother and the family needed more clothes and food from the looks of things in Anheung village.

After the shopping I had three or four thousand dollars left. The Party official suggested that I leave it behind on behalf of the family. I had in mind to do exactly the same when he suggested it, and I gave him the money with a condition that they move my mother and the family to Pyongyang. I also asked him to enroll my nephew in Kim Il Sung University or equivalent in Pyongyang.

Throughout my visit, I was generous with my dollars to anyone and everyone, whomever I thought could help my mother and the family. I gave money gifts to the guides, the Party officials in Pyongyang, and the local officials in my mother's village. With just two dollars, they could exchange for local currency the equivalent to the monthly salary of an average worker. A ten, twenty, or one hundred-dollar bill went a long way in garnering goodwill in the society I knew very little of, and I was glad that I had the money to pass around. I wasn't thinking of the politics, the ideology, or the social structure of the society. I was only focusing on the welfare of my mother and the family, and I made that fact very plain to whomever I talked to.

Back in the States, it was difficult to explain my situation to those who grew up in the free society of America. PACO customers and friends were happy for me that I had found my mother after forty years. They asked me many questions about the strange country my mother lived in, and I answered the questions as carefully as I could.

I say carefully because I didn't want any negative comments getting back to North Korea, although it seemed very unlikely that any of my conversations in the States would be ferried across the Pacific to cause harm to my mother. But I couldn't take that chance. People asked me, "Why don't you bring her here?"

I explained to them that it would take an act of Congress, maybe more, to bring her out of the country where everyone is a closely guarded subject of the state. She wasn't free to come and go as she wished.

Let me give you an idea how the travelling system works over there. Say, you want to go from Wonsan to Pyongyang about one hundred miles away. You figure out when and where you want to go and make an application for a travel permit at the government office in your district in Wonsan, filling out your name, address, destination, the names of the persons you plan to visit, their addresses, the dates and so forth. Your district office in Wonsan sends your application to the district office in Pyongyang, which then investigates the persons you plan to visit and the purpose of the visit. After the investigation, the Pyongyang office puts its stamp on the application and sends it back to the Wonsan office and the Wonsan office issues a travel permit. Now you're ready to buy a train ticket or a bus ticket. There's no such thing as jumping in the car in Los Angeles and drive to Santa Barbara whenever you want to. Only the high echelon of the Labor Party have cars in the first place and they can go around as they wish, but not the common folks. If you get caught without papers you're in for a lot of trouble. Even if you succeed in getting through the dragnet of the watchful eyes everywhere and manage to travel without papers, you can't escape the tight web cast over the entire society. Two, three days after you leave your home, the district or the precinct office would notice your absence and bring on wrath after wrath upon your family members, including capital punishment and banishment.

My mother and the family had been labeled "traitors" all these years, owing to my father's anti-communism activities forty years before. She had lost her husband to the firing squad and she had thought that I was gone for sure, never even telling anyone of my existence. As far as she was concerned, I had disappeared forever after the final meeting with Young-ik, my brother. Now Young-ik was missing, presumed dead, and so was Young-soo, my other brother. She had not heard from Young-soo ever since he had begun his tour of duty in the army.

She had taken on more than her share of the burden this world had to offer, and she came through like a champ bringing up the little ones in the harshest conditions I couldn't even fathom. She was evicted from her own home and the farm. She was relocated to a shack in backward area miles away from roads and civilization, living on the government's food rationing program. On a good day the rations amounted to about 300 grams (2/3 of a pound) of rice and corn per day, less for seniors and little children. On special occasions like New Years Day and Kim Il Sung's birthday, the rations included 150 grams or so of beef or pork. She planted vegetables and picked herbs around the hills for her children and herself to supplement the meager rations, and her life had not been a picnic. Nevertheless she made it, and I marveled at her resilience.

Her resilience was passed on to me along with the gift of life, and she had been with me all along through the tough times in South Korea and America. Of course, my struggles are pale compared to what she had gone through and I hoped that I had come to her as a reward for her travails.

I meant to lighten her load, for she deserved a rest. I wanted to bring her to my own peninsula called Palos

Verdes overlooking the shiny Pacific by day and the countless lights twinkling over Los Angeles basin by night. I wanted to take her for a lazy stroll on the street we live on along
with her grandchildren that she had never seen. Marilyn was
a 27-year-old lawyer now, Nelson, a 26-year-old graduate
engineer, and David, a recent graduate from engineering
school. Mother had a lot to catch up on with the grandchildren who grew up in the other end of the world. Here, she
wouldn't have to stand in line for the weekly ration. The
only line she would have to stand in was at Starbucks, trying to decide on grande Latte or tall Mocha and grumble
about the long wait just like the rest of us. She wouldn't
have to scour the hills for herbs and firewood. We could go
on outings in my Mercedes Benz to Grand Canyon or
Yosemite any time we wanted.

I wanted very much to share the life of luxury with her
and I looked into the ways to bring her out of North Korea,
the country where international travelling was unthinkable
for the common folks. Going out of the country is very rare
unless you're in the government business. That's how it is
over there. The government tells you where to go, where to
live, what to eat, and how much.

First, I checked with the State Department for the possibility of bringing my mother. They said that it was possible even though the U.S. didn't have a diplomatic relations with North Korea. The problem rested with the government of North Korea, and the permission looked doubtful. I needed to go over there if anything were to materialize, and it took another six years before another opportunity came.

In December 1994, a call came from Washington D.C. by a gentleman named J. Zumwalt, former Joint Chief of Staff for the Nixon administration and now a consultant for the government. The General introduced himself over the telephone and said, "I would like to talk to you about the American Investment Council for North Korea and the upcoming visit to North Korea in January."

"North Korea?" I replied with a question. I was surprised to hear the General talk about going to North Korea because the newspapers had been filled with the alarming news about the North Korean nuclear reactor facility and their attempt to build a nuclear bomb. The tension had been very high in the U.S., South Korea, and Japan over Kim Jong Il's pet project of developing a nuclear bomb, and he was telling me about an economic assistance for the sworn enemy. I asked him, "So, what do you want to talk about?"

"I was wondering if you could join the team of representatives for the visit."

"Me? A representative? Thank you for the invitation. I would like to talk to you more about it face to face."

"Okay. Could you come here to Washington?"

I said yes and flew to the Capital with David a few days later. On the way there, I wondered how the General had gotten hold of my name. I should have asked him but I didn't. I was only guessing that he saw my name from the list of people who had visited the White House for President Clinton's Asian American Economic Council in the spring that year. I had joined the number of Asian American business leaders in the White House, and I figured that the list was floating around somewhere and it ended up on the General's desk. I supposed also that all the accolades I had received went towards being selected for the White House council on economics, a recognition that I never dreamed of.

General Zumwalt was a kind looking man, contrary to my preconceived notion of a soldier. He greeted me warmly and explained the situation that had arisen out of the Geneva Conference held a while back between the U.S. and North Korea. The delegation was made up of fourteen members plus six other individuals in various capacities. The General said that I was nominated to represent the Asian

American business leaders and that the project would prove beneficial for me personally.

I told him about myself and added, "As you already know, I came from the North. My participation in the conference would be meaningful not only for my business but for personal reason as well. I would like to see my mother and my brother if I agree to go. Is it possible to confirm it with the North Korea government beforehand?"

General Zumwalt thought about it for a while and he promised that he would do his best to make it happen. Following the meeting, the General made several contacts with his counterpart in North Korea regarding my request. He called me a week or so later and told me about the reply he had received from the North. They had agreed in principle to my reunion with the family under the condition that neither side make any announcement to the media. That was about all anyone could expect out of North Korea. Their reply wasn't as definitive as I would have liked, especially about locating my missing brother Young-ik, who had not been heard from ever since his incarceration. The General thought that the possibility was good, and I agreed to join the delegation.

chapter 22

ECONOMIC DELEGATION

Seeing my family was number one priority for me, yet I looked forward to representing American interests as well as helping North Korea with its economy. North Korean economy had begun its slide around 1990 followed by the bad harvest in 1992 and the negative GNP year after year. I had been very concerned about the bad news coming out of North Korea, imagining the worst about the living conditions for my mother and the family. I cringed when I heard about the "Let's eat two meals a day!" campaign in the North.

Meanwhile the North Korean nuclear issue kept popping up in newspapers and on television, surrounding the ejection of IAEA (International Atomic Energy Agency) inspectors from Yong Byun nuclear processing plant. The American-North Korean relationship reached a crisis level with the talk of international sanctions against North Korea. This was not good at all. Then Time magazine and CBS News came out with a nationwide poll, which said that 51 percent of the Americans favored military action to get rid of the nuclear facility. Bombing the nuclear plant was definitely not a good idea because of the radioactive fallout that would harm my mother and the family.

There had to be a better way, and Jimmy Carter found the way. He went to Pyongyang and met with Kim Il Sung. They worked out a solution whereby Pyongyang would freeze the nuclear program, and the U.S. would drop the sanctions and the plans for a general war. I was very happy to see Jimmy Carter proclaim, "I personally believe the crisis is over." That was June 1994, and Washington announced that the third round of the U.S.-North Korea negotiations would continue in Geneva on July 8th. This was the best sign of hope for peace, especially in light of Jimmy Carter's effort in brokering a summit meeting in Pyongyang between Kim Il Sung from the North and Kim Young Sam from the South.

As fate would have it, Kim Il Sung passed away on July 8th, and the Geneva talks were postponed while North Korea mourned the death of their god-like hero. The future of the Korean Peninsula slipped into the state of quagmire once again with the South Korean armed forces going on maximum alert, and I felt nervous and helpless.

What next?

With the world watching, the Geneva Conference picked up again in August 1994, and the U.S. and North Korea signed an accord in October. I was happy to see both parties settle down finally after all the threats of quitting the negotiations back and forth, and with Kim Young Sam grumbling about leaving South Korea out of the negotiations in his interview with the New York Times. I supposed that the President of South Korea had a point in saying that the northern regime was on the brink of collapse, and that the Geneva talks gave North Korea a new lease on life.

A lot of people thought that the U.S. negotiators gave away too much, but I was just glad that it was over. The U.S. got what they wanted—freezing all the activities on the existing nuclear reactors and eventually replacing the plutonium producing reactors with new light-water reactors. North Korea got what they wanted—a nuclear plant, heavy oil fuel and the start for the normalization process with the U.S.

As part of the normalization process, the White House appointed General Zumwalt as the principal coordinator for organizing an American delegation for the Pyongyang trip. This was where I came on the scene when General Zumwalt called me in December.

International politics was not on my mind. I was excited about seeing my mother and the prospect of finding Young-ik. Sue got busy shopping for my mother and packed a trunk load of clothes, foodstuff, and trinkets for me to take to Pyongyang. Early February 1995, I left for Beijing, where all the delegates were to meet. I met the rest of the delegation at the Beijing Hotel. They were mostly businessmen representing various industries like telecommunication, steel, shipbuilding, automobile, banking, garment, and construction sectors. PACO represented the steel industry, along with Thyssen Rheinstahl, a German steelworks company. There were several scholars and reporters as well.

We received a briefing from the State Department and the intelligence people regarding the mission. They conducted seminars on the U.S.-North Korea relationship, the Geneva talks, and the reduction of trade barriers and investments between the two countries.

Our delegation was a precursor to the formal economic cooperation and we were to study the economic conditions of North Korea and search for the potential items that we could cooperate on. Jim Zumwalt Jr., General Zumwalt's son and a long-time attorney with the State Department headed up the delegation. He talked about the North Korean economy, the socialist system versus the American market system. In North Korea, he said, the government owns everything, the land, the houses, the schools, the hospitals, the factories and the farms. There was no such thing as private property other than immediate contents in the homes. He went on to describe the economic structure, which I was familiar with, but it was new to the rest of the delegation. He concluded by saying, "We are not here to make deals or to sign contracts. We're interested in producing M.O.U. (Memorandum of Understanding) on a case-by-case basis. That's the extent of our mission."

We arrived in Pyongyang on February 14, 1995. I felt like a homecoming hero, returning home with a team of world-class businessmen and investors to help my mother, my mother's country and its battered economy. I was returning as a member of the peaceful mission from America with investors who could change the living conditions for the better. As we were greeted by the North Korean delegation at the airport, I was thinking good thoughts about the future, the thawing of the relations between America and

North Korea.

The first order of business was the visit to Kim Il Sung's statue. The North Korean counterparts lined up in front of the statue and bowed 90 degrees to their departed Great Leader. The American delegation stood in a moment of silence in the usual show of respect.

We were driven to the VIP guesthouse next. There was nothing on the agenda that evening, and I unpacked the luggage in leisure, followed by a dinner in the dining room. After dinner, one of the guides brought me the news I had been waiting for. He said, "You are set to spend three days with your family after the conference."

I was in heaven.

I was up early the next morning, anxious to tackle the business of economic cooperation that would lead to better conditions for my mother and the family and the rest of the country. The day started with a quick breakfast and a ride to the People's Cultural Palace. I entered in my diary:

February 15, 1995

We were driven to the People's Cultural Palace in the morning for the first session. Foreign Cooperation Committee Secretary-General Kim Mun Sung opened the session with a welcoming remark for the American delegation, and the head of the American delegation [Jim] Zumwalt replied with the congratulatory remarks for Kim Jong Il's 53rd birthday and presented a bouquet of flowers. The American delegation consisted of 19 delegates, ten Caucasians and nine Asian origin from Hong Kong, Japan, Malaysia, Laos, and me.

North Korean side consisted of Secretary-General Kim Mun Sung, the translator, and the representatives from various industries. Kim Mun Sung said, "Three, four years ago our Great Leader Kim Il Sung embarked on the international trading in Najin region, but it was put on hold because of the threat of a war during the [Geneva] Conference. I am happy to see that the U.S.-North Korea relations is on a friendly course."

Zumwalt replied that the Great Leader had a vision, but unfortunately he passed away without seeing its results. Fortunately, however, the American delegation made it here, and he asked us to introduce ourselves individually.

We took turns introducing ourselves, and the North Korean translator translated. When my turn came, I asked the American delegation if it was all right to speak Korean. They said it was all right and I spoke in Korean.

I said, "As you can see, I am Korean. You might find it odd that a Korean like myself is part of the American delegation. But that is America. America is a diversified society where many different nationalities live together. The delegation reflects the American diversity. Born in Sungchun in Pyong Nam Province, I went to America with nothing, went to a university, and built a business with my own hands. America is a wonderful country where opportunities exist for everyone. I am honored for the opportunity to come here as a member of the American delegation and see what I could do for my fatherland. I own and operate the largest company in the field of light steel industry. My area covers from steel production to distribution. I look forward to the good U.S.-North Korea relations and I would like to contribute what I can in this area."

I thought I made a good speech, considering all the appropriate elements, but the reaction from the North Korean side was rather cool, which surprised me. I wondered what they were thinking. Did they feel hostile toward me, a person who had escaped away from their reign and made good in the enemy country? Was I not a participant in improving the relations? Or, did they feel awkward in seeing a son of a traitor return as an American delegate? Whatever they felt, I figured that it was complex, as complex as my own ambivalence about lending a hand to the regime that was unkind to my family. But I didn't look back. I didn't want to outguess them or myself. Strong emotions from our history only cluttered up the ability to think, and I sat down in my seat as I said, "Thank you."

After the introductions, the head of North Korean delegation Kim Jung Wu addressed the American delegation, "The economic climate in North Korea is changing. We invite you to utilize our superior labor force and trust the political stability and invest freely."

The afternoon session focused on the specific industries, and I was matched up with Ahn Soo-il, the North Korean representative in the steel industry sector. Mr. Ahn and his staff showed a lot of interest in PACO. He began by saying, "We have an urgent need to develop the steel sector. Please help us. I'm really proud that you're Korean."

My talks with Mr. Ahn went very well. He was 65 years old, born in Hamkyung Province. He went to Moscow University and devoted his life to the steel industry. He talked proudly about his three children, all of them university graduates. He talked about the steel products out of their steel mill in Kim Chaek, the hot coil, H-beams, and the rolling mill. He said that Kim Il Sung had directed them to produce 100,000 tons of steel products per year, but it took a tremendous amount of capital. The committee had suggested that a proposal for a new mill in Najin be included in the agenda, and Mr. Ahn was most anxious to work on it. I discussed the mill, recommending to use the Kyoei Steel plant model from Japan. I also suggested a steel technology center in Najin. All in all, our discussions were open and frank, and I enjoyed exchanging ideas with the group. We agreed to draw up an M.O.U. based on our discussions.

The only time Mr. Ahn raised his voice was when he

talked about South Korea. He was angry about the way Kim Young Sam behaved when Kim Il Sung passed away, complaining bitterly that the South Korean president didn't send one word of condolence. Kim Il Sung had passed away in the midst of preparing for the historical summit with Kim Young Sam, directing all the details of the reception himself. In fact, on the day he passed away, Kim Il Sung was inspecting the guest villa in Myohyang Mountains, about 100 miles north of Pyongyang, where Kim Young Sam was to stay. He had spent a hot, exhaustive day, which led to a massive heart attack. The otherwise quiet and gentleman, Mr. Ahn bellowed, "That heartless Kim Young Sam ordered the South Korean military on alert and prepared for an invasion instead of expressing condolence!" He had kind words for Bill Clinton, grateful for the telegram from the White House.

When I wasn't meeting with Mr. Ahn and his staff, I spent time with GM's Tom McDaniel and his North Korean counterparts. GM was interested in assembling cars in North Korea for exporting to South Korea and China, and I facilitated the talks between them.

Tom McDaniel asked the North Korean counterparts specific questions about taxation. "If GM comes into North

Korea, are there going to be taxes?"

North Korean delegate answered, "No."

"When we export cars to China from here are there going to be taxes?"

"No."

"When we export cars to South Korea from here are there going to be taxes?"

"No."

Tom McDaniel liked what he was hearing. He beamed wide and began talking to me like he had found a long-lost cousin. "This is good news. What I'm seeing here is the low labor cost, land access, and now they're telling me no tax. We can compete with Hyundai cars as long as there's no tax. This is very exciting. It's worth looking into." He and I went on like this for a while with the North Korean officials looking on. They probably didn't understand what we were talking about other than the fact that a big shot from GM was excited about what they had said. I couldn't translate everything Tom was saying because he was talking too fast.

I turned to the North Korean officials and told them that GM's total business volume was larger than all the South Korean exports combined together. If GM were a country its economy would be ranked number 13 in the world. They couldn't imagine such a huge company, and I said, "Neither can I." I told them that they should hang on to GM no matter what the condition and that others would follow. The North Korean official held my hand and asked, "Mr. Paik, please help us."

I told them that I would.

In the end, the talk with GM didn't amount to anything specific because of the lack of the follow-up procedure on the part of the North Korean officials. The General Motors took it as a sign of disinterest, I thought. It could have been a win-win situation for both sides, and I hated to see any potential win-win deal lose its steam. The North Korean delegates saw how easily I communicated with Tom McDaniel and they saw the value in my rapport with the GM executive.

But they didn't know how to pursue my rapport with GM, nor did they know how to secure my help. They should have found out what I really wanted. By the same token, they should have pursued what GM really wanted, its goals, its approach, and its history. They should have found out about everything about GM, but they didn't do the necessary homework to put down something concrete on the table for GM to hang on to.

Getting help from me would have been a simple matter,

for all I wanted was to see my mother and my brother. Maybe they knew it but they didn't believe it. Maybe they were caught up in their own bureaucracy, the sense of importance for their own mission. If they had taken the trouble to realize my own mission in life and respected it, I would have done everything for them.

But they did the opposite. At the farewell dinner with all the dignitaries in attendance, I was enjoying the relaxed atmosphere filled with good will, exchanging MOU's followed by applause and toasts.

Privately, I was looking forward to spending three days with my mother and possibly my brother after the conference. At about ten in the evening, a messenger came to my table and told me, "Go home with the American delegation tomorrow. A high official will meet you at the airport and explain the situation to you." And he hurried off.

Imagine my shock, my mouth dropped as I watched the man disappear among the tables. I turned to the table where the chief North Korean delegate was seated and I blurted out loudly in Korean, "Is this true?" I think I said it once more, "Is this true?"

The hall went silent, and the chief North Korean delegate looked at me and then his colleagues and they started talking fast among themselves. Finally, Kim Mun Sung said to me, "We'll make some calls and find out what's going on."

Zumwalt and the American delegates wanted to know what was going on and I said plaintively, "They told me that I can't meet my family. What the hell is going on!"

Zumwalt and the American delegates started to talk among themselves, buzzing about keeping promises and shaking their heads with sour faces. The American delegates were disgusted and they joined in on the protest, producing a letter to pull out of all the agreements and MOU's written up so far.

Kim Mun Sung told me to be patient repeatedly while his people made some telephone calls, and I waited, dejected and angry. They came back with the same story: "Some high official will explain everything to you at the airport tomorrow. All you have to do is rest well tonight and go to the airport tomorrow."

"I don't understand any of this!" I yelled, but they didn't know any better, or they had said all they were going to say about it. I turned around and went to my room. I wasn't doing much good throwing a tantrum in the middle of the international conference. It would have been easy for me to stay and blast them for reneging on the promise and put on the gloves along with the American delegation, who, by now, were fully agitated. In life a person gets to choose battles, and at sixty-five, I'd had a handful of opportunities. But this one was a battle to choose very carefully because I had too much at stake, the welfare of my mother and the family, and I backed off.

In the hotel room I packed my bags. The lights went dead in my room at irregular intervals, and I jumped and cussed each time the darkness invaded the room and the entire cityscape outside the window. I lit the candles that came with the room, reminding myself that electricity was not to be taken for granted there, the condition that had existed before I left the country. I had become accustomed to having lights long since then, and when I turned on the light switch I expected to see light. I felt as though I had traveled back in time and landed on a strange planet, not my homeland, the place of my birth that held the memories of my happy childhood and my youth filled with promises. But I was far, far away from all those things. The time and place that I cherished had disappeared now as though they had never existed, an illusion. Hadn't I run home from school to push the rickety gate in and yell, "Mother, I'm home!" and stuck my head into the kitchen and taken a whiff at the sweet stew mother was cooking? Didn't I toss my school bag into the room and run out to the street and play with the village kids until mother called me for dinner? I kept on playing, saying, "I'll be right in, mother!" and mother called me in again and I said, "I'll be right in!" a few more times to the point when her voice told me that there wasn't going to be any dinner for me if I didn't go in right then. Was it all a mirage? A dream? False memory?

A giant shadow stood in my way, telling me that I couldn't see my mother, and something was very wrong in this world. I could understand that electricity was not to be taken for granted, but I couldn't understand their turning off the switch on my mother.

chapter 23

HWANG JANG-YOP

February 18, 1995

All the [American] delegates mustered at eight in the morning. Just before we departed [the hotel] a red Benz appeared in front of us and a man told me to get in the car. Sudden separation from the group made me uneasy, but I obliged, having no choice in the matter. Kim Duk-hong was in the car waiting and he said, "Party Secretary Hwang Jang-yop and Commerce Vice Chairman Shin Hyun-gul are waiting for you in the VIP room at the airport. This time, your family reunion is impossible. The Commerce Ministry turned it over to the Party just yesterday and we don't have time to arrange it... Please don't worry about it this time, we'll make a special arrangement for your family next time. And I will deliver your mother's luggage for you. There aren't any 'Made-in-Korea' labels, are there? Oh, yes, Comrade Hwang Jang-yop has high respect for Dosan Ahn Chang Ho."

I relaxed a bit after the meeting with Hwang Jang-yop. Hwang Jang-yop asked me to send him books on Dosan. As we parted, I asked Kim Duk-hong to look after my family. I boarded the airplane with a VIP send-off. I told Zumwalt and Samboon that everything was okay. We left for Beijing.

Hwang Jang-yop impressed me as a spirited scholar as he greeted me cordially when I met him at the airport. "Welcome, Mr. Paik, I appreciate your long journey here." He looked sincere and trustworthy, putting me at ease right away. He proceeded to explain the situation to me. "We learned that you are a respected businessman in America with considerable influence. I would like to extend my personal invitation for you to come back in the near future for a proper reunion with your family, rather than trying to arrange a hurried meeting as an afterthought. I would like to ask for your understanding this time and to return home without worries. Kim Duk-hong, my assistant, will handle our communication from here on, and I would like to ask for your cooperation. I will be sending you a message soon."

Hearing this, I opened up to him. "Frankly, I would like to find out about my brother than anything else at this point. Ever since I left my brother behind every living moment was a torture for me. The reason I came with the American delegation was because of my brother. If you let me meet with my brother I will do anything. Please find my brother for me."

He replied, "Leave it to us. We'll find out what happened to him." These words came from the man who held the second highest office next only to Kim Jong Il, and I believed that he could find my brother if anyone could. Hwang Jang-yop was the man who had helped Kim Il Sung with the Ju Che (Self Reliance) doctrine, which later became the basis for governing the country for four decades.

Hwang Jang-yop kept his promise. He sent an invitation in August and I arrived in Beijing on September 14th. Kim Duk-hong was there to meet me, and I had dinner with him and others, mostly talking about the changing North Korean economy. They were devoted to Hwang Jang-yop and his ideas in moving the economy towards the free market system. They said, "Only Hwang Jang-yop can lead us to the free market system, and we'll achieve it in two to three years. The perception towards the businessman is changing.

If a man buys fish for a dollar on the East Coast and sells the fish for fifteen dollars in Pyongyang, the practice is accepted now despite the windfall profit. He used to be scorned upon as a profiteer or a carpetbagger, but now he is looked upon as a man who is doing a service for the society. This is the road to the ultimate unification [between the South and the North]. The Party is still resisting the truth and it has a lot of problems, but the free market will win out in the end because it is the true way. Hwang Jang-yop will lead us to it and we will serve him with our lives."

This was a new revelation for me. I recalled the newspaper report of pollack fish rotting in Wonsan port every year, a problem that was attributed to the lack of transportation. But now I saw that the report was superficial. The problem went deeper. In a market economy, people would have found ways to transport the pollack fish to Pyongyang market for the kind of profit Kim and his colleagues were referring to. The price would have stabilized eventually, and the popular fish would never rot at the port. It made good sense that they were thinking about the market economy to close the gap between Pyongyang and the rest of the country.

Socialism isn't worth beans as far as I am concerned, and I thought that North Korea needed to move away from it and engage the population in the overall economic activity in order to survive. There was no recognizable economic structure there, nothing like anyone had seen around here in the States. The condition wasn't going to change overnight though, and all the talking about the big picture was only good for passing the time. My concerns were more immediate: how do I make things better for my mother and how do I find my brother?

As an outsider, I needed to understand what was going on in North Korea in order to help my mother and the family and I listened to everything they had to say about the society. In a nutshell, Pyongyang was the place to be. It had dollar-based department stores there and you can buy Sony television sets, Armani suits, Polo shirts, and Italian shoes as long as you had dollars to spend. There were fancy restaurants where you could dine in gourmet style with French wine and top it off with expensive brandy and a Havana cigar. Pyongyang had money to burn, enough to shell out $15 for a pollack fish, which shouldn't cost any more than $1. I asked what was going on there, and they replied matter-of-factly, "That's the elite economy reserved for the upper crust Party members. They have their own economy and they're not affected by the general economy. After that, the military has the priority in food, clothes and supplies. Whatever is left over goes to the general public."

They were talking about a class system that was connected to the economic system, and the whole concept didn't register with me right away. As they talked I had to remind myself that government owned everything in a socialist system and that the government told everyone where to live, work, and send their children to school. In distributing the wealth, the government classified the population into five distinct categories, not unlike the ancient noble system.

The pecking order went like this: The first category consisted of the families related to the revolutionaries, Kim Il Sung's comrades during the Japanese occupation in Korea before World War II. The second tier was assigned to those who had distinguished themselves during the People's War (Korean War) and their families. Then came the third class, the plain average people. The fourth tier belonged to the traitors and their families. The fifth tier was made up of retarded people.

Like I said, the first tier lived well without knowing any economic limitation. The state assigned the biggest houses for them in Pyongyang, cars, and the best schools for their children. The military echelon and their families lived comfortably in Pyongyang as well, unaffected by the recent shortages.

The struggle began with the third class, the average people without Party affiliation, lower rank military, working stiffs, teachers, factory workers, clerks, most of who lived on rationed food with the average salary of about 100 won per month. The official exchange rate was around 15 won to one dollar. So, we're looking at around six dollars and change for them to live on for a month, and that's pitiful even with the government housing and the food ration.

My mother and the family belonged in the fourth tier according to the official scheme of things, which put her below-poverty level, save for the money I had spread around six years ago plus the money I had left seven months before. She and the family had lived comfortably, independent of the class system and way above average, and I was glad that I could do that much at least. I meant to do more for them, like moving them to Pyongyang to start. I arrived in Pyongyang airport with the new resolve and the excitement of seeing my mother and the prospect of finding Young-ik.

I checked into the VIP guest house on September 16, and Hwang Jang-yop brought mother in his Benz next day. We went to my room, and we sat down. What Hwang Jang-yop did next shocked me. He stood up in front of my mother and gave her a traditional bow, on his knees with his hands on the floor and his forehead on the hands. I was speechless at the act of ultimate respect, but mother took it in stride. She leaned over and said, "Thank you very much for bringing my son," into his ear.

chapter 24

MOTHER'S TEARS

After Hwang Jang-yop left, mother began crying. She hadn't cried at all during my last trip, which struck me rather odd then. But she didn't hold back her tears this time. She began with the day father was shot and she didn't stop. "I buried him," she said, "but I don't remember where exactly and it will be hard for me to find it."

I protested, "But they took me to father's grave last time."

She continued, "It's all a lie. Nobody knows where. It was at nighttime, and I took the children and we went to your sister's house. Then I was sent to Pyongyang to do the clean-up work after the bombing."

She lived there during the war. Young-ik joined the military and learned to be a mechanic. After the discharge, he found a good job as a mechanic and lived in Pyongyang, marrying a wonderful woman in 1962. Then suddenly, he received an order to move to Taechon and to take the rest of the family with him. Mother and everyone went there, not understanding what was happening to them. In the meantime, baby sister Soon-han turned twenty, and it was time for her to get married. Young-ik took on the responsibility to arrange her marriage, as he was the oldest son in the family then. He set out to find a groom in Pyongyang for her and he succeeded, but she needed a travel certificate to go to Pyongyang, a document similar to an unobtainable visa. Young-ik befriended the official in charge of issuing the certificate and managed to send Soon-han to Pyongyang.

For reasons not too clear to me, Young-ik's relationship with the certificate agent turned sour later, and the certificate became a source of trouble for Young-ik. The agent reported to the authorities that Young-ik had committed fraud in arranging for the travel certificate. About the same time, Young-ik had an occasion to have a drink with another friend in a tavern. The occasion turned into a grieving session for them. His friend complained bitterly about the government, the unfair and corrupt practices, and Young-ik aired his own grudges. A mole in the tavern had overheard Young-ik's friend and reported him to the authorities. Under

interrogation Young-ik's friend confessed his anti-state attitude and admitted that Young-ik had been with him when
he aired his grievance. Young-ik was in trouble for sure
then, and he worried about it for days.

On June 26, 1970, Young-ik received a notification to
come to the post office, and he left for the post office. As he
left, he said, "I'm going to the post office and I'll be back."
Those were his last words, and no one ever saw him again.
Mother and Young-ik's wife tried to find out what happened
to him, but the police and the local authorities told them
nothing. There was no one to ask, nowhere to turn to,
which is how it is in a totalitarian society. When a person
disappears out of the blue, it is assumed that he is gone for
good, especially when he is accused of espousing anti-state
ideas. It does no good to dig into the matter because one
risks his or her own welfare. Neighbors and friends did not
dare to whisper about Young-ik's disappearance for fear of
reprisal.

Young-su, my youngest brother, did not heed to the common practice of keeping quiet about Young-ik's disappearance. With Young-ik gone, Young-su became the head of
the household along with all the responsibilities of looking
after mother, Young-ik's family, and his own. After the mili-

tary service Young-su had married and lived in the same village with his older brother Young-ik.

Young-su was not one to keep quiet about Young-ik's incarceration and he challenged the authorities. "What did my old brother do wrong? Didn't he serve in the military for the country? Why did you take him away?"

The authorities didn't take too kindly to Young-su's attitude. They told him, "You, you're same as your brother. You need to spend time inside, too. You must go to the work camp!"

Young-su's crime was less serious, and he was sentenced to a camp in Hamkyung Province. Soon, a truck came for him and his wife and took them away. That was the last time mother saw him.

Mother and Young-ik's wife struggled to tell these stories, their voices choking in between sobs. Mother's tears prompted my own tears, and we wept together well into the night, the tears that we had built up over forty years.

There was only one thing left to do, which was locating Young-ik and Young-su. Mother and Young-ik's wife kept on saying, "Let's find them. Whatever it takes, let's find them. If they were dead we would have heard by now. We haven't heard that they were dead and we must find them."

I agreed with them and I checked with my contacts through Kim Duk-hong and other high officials. They replied that it was possible to see my brothers, and they added that I needed to show goodwill from my end. By goodwill, they meant a donation of one million dollars to the government, namely Kim Jong Il. A million dollars was a lot of money, but if it produced my brothers, I was ready to go along with the idea no matter how appalling it seemed to me. The idea of paying money to see my family was foreign to my way of thinking, especially when the officials pressed me hard for the money. I thought that there was something wrong because they kept up the pressure tactics for hours, asking me to make a commitment with a promissory note. What they were requesting was not my goodwill but ransom money. Besides, there was a problem of transferring funds to North Korea from the U.S., because there was no banking agreement between the two countries. Bringing in one million dollar cash was not an option, and the only way to do it was to obtain permission from the U.S. government. I wrote on a piece of paper, "I will do my best as far as the U.S. laws would allow." I signed the paper and gave it to them. They seemed to be satisfied with the note, although not completely.

It did start the ball rolling as far as I knew, and we waited for the news. In the meantime, mother, Young-ik's wife, and I went shopping across Daedong River at the Daesong department store every day, where they accepted only dollars. It was stocked with mostly Japanese goods and some Russian and Chinese products. Mother needed shoes, and I bought three or four pairs of shoes and a pair of boots for her. All in all, we bought $1,500 worth of clothes and outfits for mother and she didn't know what to think of the spree. She said, "I've never worn boots like these. When I die, I'll give them to my daughter-in-law."

I said, laughing, "Mother, they're yours. Why are you thinking about giving them away already?"

She laughed, too, and said, "Yeah, you're right. I'll take them with me when I die."

Mother's frequent references to dying were unsettling for me even though I tried to make light of it. She continued, "I'll be hundred years old in three years. When I turn one hundred, the country will give me a big reward. They will give me a full pardon for the crimes against the state. I will be free of the traitor status."

Young-ik's wife agreed, "Yes... We're all looking forward to the day."

The news of my brothers never came, as we did more shopping and went to restaurants including Ok Ryu Gwan, famous for *nangmyun*, cold buckwheat noodle soup. She said, "I'm having noodles with my son," over and over in between her toothless bites as if to remind herself that she was not in a dream. Neither one of us said anything about her other sons, my brothers, but the noodles would have tasted much better with Young-ik and Young-su there.

One evening Hwang Jang-yop arranged a dinner with his family at Ryanggang Hotel. He introduced his son to me, a fine looking young man of twenty-eight, and I liked him right away. He wore a Polo shirt, and I told him in English, "Wonderful shirt."

Hwang Kyung-mo spoke English well and he smiled wide at my reference to the American brand shirt. He replied in Korean, "I bought it because you were coming."

We continued our conversation well after dinner, and I was impressed with his intellect and openness. He gave me a rundown on his life without my asking, offering me paintings by a famous North Korean artist. I accepted the gifts gladly, and I have them hanging on my living-room walls now. The dinner cost me $697, $352 for the meal and $345 for what they called service fee. With the money for the dinner I could have bought 2,800 pounds of rice in the black market. I thought that the restaurant had made a mistake with the bill, but it turned out to be correct. I didn't know what to think then, whether they were gouging me or they were ignorant of the value of the dollar.

Waiting around for the news of my brothers was unbearable, but on the other hand, the days flew by and before I knew it, it was time for me to leave. I didn't want to leave mother behind again and I gave more thought to bringing her with me to the States. I thought through the pros and cons about her new life in America, and in the end, I concluded that she belonged in her home despite my desire to have her close to me. At ninety-six the long trip seemed prohibitive. She needed to be here to wait for my brothers' return. These were what she lived for now, turning one hundred years old and my brothers, and my wish to bring her with me seemed selfish at this point.

I said goodbye to mother once again, and she asked to see me once more before she left this world. She said, "Bring back Young-ik and Young-su to me. And help my grandsons Sung-chul and Woong-chul. I want them to turn out like you have. I have nothing more to wish for now. I can die in peace knowing that I had brought a wonderful man like you into this world."

I mumbled something to the effect that I didn't care for the way she talked alout dying, but we both knew that this was our last meeting. I put on the best face I could for her and said, "I'll see you again soon. Please stay well, mother." Over and over.

chapter 25

ARKANSAS PLANT

Back in the States, another turning point in my life waited for me. Japanese yen had been rising against the dollar, which put a financial strain on the Sumitomo steel plant. Their exporting cost skyrocketed with the rise of the yen, but they had continued to supply the beams to PACO at the contract price based on the dollar. They were losing their shirts, and they wanted to cut back their production. Better yet, they wanted to get out of the business altogether. I pleaded with them to hang on, but the situation became intolerable for them.

I turned to Chaparral and Nucor more than before and I began thinking about building a plant in the States, especially for the corrugated beams. I sensed that it was time for me to go on my own and manufacture my own beams rather than depending on Sumitomo. I told Sumitomo Steel of my plans to build a plant in the States and asked for their participation.

They jumped at the idea. "Let's get Nomura Trading involved also. The three of us can renegotiate our relations and build the factory together." Sumitomo and Nomura formed a team together right away, and came to Los Angeles for the project planning. We went to work on the list of items, land, building facility, equipment, supplies, staff, operating capital, and so forth. When we added up everything, we were looking at a hefty budget of almost $100 million. Sumitomo and Nomura agreed to put up two-thirds, and I agreed to put up one-third of the required capitalization with a bank loan.

As expected, it took us a long time to iron out the investment strategy, but all the parties agreed principally with the plan. Then came the details. As the majority shareholder of the project, Sumitomo wanted to bring in their own equipment, their own technology, as well as their own people to manage the operation. I supposed that they had a right to propose such an arrangement, but it didn't sit well with me. It seemed one-sided in favor of the Japanese partners, leaving only a cursory role for PACO. I re-examined the arrangement and concluded that I would end up giving them money and PACO's name for very little control. Something was off-balance, I thought, because the whole idea of building a plant in the States was to make my life easier, not the other way around. I wanted control over production to facilitate the sales and marketing effort. The customer was king, and I wanted everything to flow from that principle. I asked my financial consulting firm to figure out a better way. They went to work, looking at the assets, the market condition, and the future potential in detail, and they came back with a conclusion that I had enough assets to fly on my own and that I didn't need to do the joint venture with the Japanese. I was surprised to hear that, and when they told me that they would arrange the loan for the project, I said, yes. I told the Japanese partners that I was going on my own and went to work on building the plant.

During my travels throughout the States, nothing impressed me more than the Mississippi River and the Missouri River and the tributary feeders like the Ohio and Arkansas River. The artery system was a lifeline, and it made sense to place a factory near the proven delivery system. Aside from the water transportation, trucking was an important factor as well. Arkansas was the well-known hub for a trucking system. It so happened that Arkansas was central to the majority of my customers in Georgia and Texas. The State of Arkansas was attracting steel mills and the associated industries, and Nucor Steel was one of them. In terms of size, Nucor was number two next to US Steel but number one in profit. Nucor's Arkansas plant produced the best hot coil at the best price, and its management offered me the rolled products and asked me to come to Arkansas. So Arkansas became the home of the new PACO plant. I bought an old cotton farm, a 34-acre plot next to the Nucor plant, and began constructing the factory.

It was completed in September 1997, and it went on production. I felt proud to see PACO beams roll off the production line, my own corrugated beams made in the US of A. PACO was not just a distributor any more. PACO became a true steel company, and it was a long time coming.

chapter 26

ENTREPRENEUR OF THE YEAR

It took another year or so for the Arkansas plant to reach the full capacity, longer than I had expected. Nevertheless, I welcomed the inventory because we needed them badly. Business was good, and the demand for light steel beams soared, creating short supply in the overall marketplace.

At a glance, this condition may appear to be the ideal situation for any businessman, but I don't see it that way. My first and foremost concern is for the customers' needs, good price and smooth delivery schedule, and I don't like to put any strain on the customer's routine that they work so hard to achieve. Shortage is my problem, not the customer's, and it is simply wrong to tell a customer, "I can put you on the waiting list," or raise the price. I search all over the world to bring good products for good prices and that's how I maintain my customer base. In a free market system, it's bad for the market to dry up, obviously. On the other hand, excessive demand brings on other problems, like new competition.

Sure enough, Nucor was looking into entering the light steel beam market around 1998, and I knew that their presence was going be a thorn in my side. With their huge resources they could put a dent in the market even though their main business was in the heavy steel beams. So when Chaparral proposed to increase the price and take advantage of the good business climate, I didn't go along with the idea. We could have gotten away with it, but it was one sure way to violate the customers' trust.

I proposed to keep the price the same and to reduce the market share downward from 60 percent to make room for Nucor. Going head-to-head against a big player like Nucor would have cost PACO and Chaparral dearly.

Chaparral balked at my idea. "If you handle Nucor products, we're going to break off our relationship with PACO," they said.

I pointed out to Chaparral management Nucor's arsenal, the capital, the ingot mill, the production capacity, all of which pointed to lower cost and lower price to customers.

Nucor was going to have its market share whether we liked it or not.

But Chaparral didn't see it that way. Chaparral and Nucor had been butting heads in the heavy beam market for years, and sharing the market with an arch enemy didn't sit well with the folks at Chaparral. They floated the idea of buying PACO outright.

Selling PACO was out of the question, I told them.

Chaparral ended the dialog by cutting off PACO. I didn't want to see things go that way with Chaparral and their stubborn tactics. Without Chaparral's products, PACO was put on the spot, but it wasn't the end of the road, thanks to the Arkansas plant. I had to scramble around to make up the inventory, that was all.

In the meantime, Nucor did their market research and concluded that PACO was the key distributor for their new line of products. They asked me to handle the sales and distribution of the light beams for them, and I agreed.

So, the dust settled with PACO and Chaparral going our separate ways. These things happen in all business endeavors, and I wish the best for them.

No matter what, the market behavior and the mood of the customer determine what we do, the competition and the price structure. Manufacturers do not decide the price like in the old days, and I will never forget that.

Apparently, a lot of folks in the business world thought that I knew what I was doing. Ernst & Young, a reputable accounting firm, picked me out of the crowd and recognized me as The Entrepreneur Of the Year for 1999-2000. I had no idea what EOY was, nor did I know that it was such a big deal sponsored by CNN, USA Today, Citibank, and NASDAQ.

On November 1, 1999, Sue and I got all dressed up in our Palm Springs condo and went to a black tie ceremony at Palm Springs Marriott with about 3,000 entrepreneurs attending from all over the world. The EOY committee presented me with an award that had gone to the likes of Ted Turner and Bill Gates, and I wondered if they had made a mistake

in selecting me. Sue and I had talked about whether we should attend the ceremony or not. After some discussion we decided to go there just to see what it was like, never dreaming that I would win the coveted award over other well-known candidates in the Manufacturing Sector. When Jack Stack, the Master of Ceremonies and a famous entrepreneur and an author, called out my name, I couldn't believe my ears. I looked at Sue—she was in  shock—and I gave her a hug. Jack made the introduction with such glowing accolades that I didn't recognize the person he was referring to. He was talking about me in front of all those achievers in the business world, and I wanted him to stop exaggerating. Yet I took the trophy as recognition for my efforts through the years and I felt like I was on top of the world.

With music and champagne all around us, I looked at Sue and she looked at me and we said, "We've come a long way from the Lakeshore days in Chicago." Sue, my partner in life and business, wept happy tears. "This is yours," I said and handed her the trophy.

I wanted to share the award with one other person. My brother Young-ik.

I had just come from Seoul a week before, where I met Hwang Jang-yop. I never dreamt that I would see him in Seoul, the opposite end of Pyongyang. His defection from North Korea was big news around the world amidst the North Korean accusation that South Korea had abducted Hwang, the venerable mentor to Kim Jong Il.

In a heavily guarded safe house in Seoul, he wept for his family. "I am a bad, horrible sinner, leaving behind my family." By a strange twist of fate and politics, former number two man next to Kim Il Sung and I found ourselves together, lamenting about our respective families we had left behind. He told me what happened to Young-ik. Haltingly, Hwang Jang-yop said, "Your brother was arrested many years ago. In North Korea, they execute inmates not for their own crimes, but for some other crimes. So your brother passed away in those circumstances. He passed away a long time ago. Only Kim Jong Il knew about it..."

chapter 27

YENZI

Hwang Jang-yop's words rang in my ears for a long time. The words gave me the final closure to Young-ik's life, and I was relieved to know his fate one way or the other. Not knowing had caused years of nightmares. After the relief passed, however, I became bitter and angry. I found myself pacing at home and at work, frequently hollering "How could they do this!" at random intervals. Other times, I went on quiet tirades, not looking at or talking to anyone for long stretches of time.

My angst about Young-ik dampened my euphoria over the Entrepreneur of the Year award. No award—no matter how prestigious—was a match for my time with Young-ik.

Then a letter came from Young-ik's wife in march 2000. It bore the news that mother had passed away. Needless to say, I was shocked at first, but I became numb as time went on.

Strange enough, my angst over Young-ik subsided as we prepared a service for mother at my home. Thanks to the church members and their help, I was able to take my mind off Young-ik for a while.

Sue helped me through these tough times. She reminded me that there was nothing I could do for him now other than try to cherish the good memories, no matter how scant they might be. Whatever the evil spirit that had led my brother to his demise, I couldn't let it overtake me, too, she said. She was right, I knew, but I struggled to fight off the temptation to let the bitterness get the best of me. Vengeful thoughts came so much easier than reconstructing Young-ik whole in my mind. Ultimately, I chose the latter. I refused to let Young-ik fall victim to the inhumane world. I turned to what I do best, which is building dreams, and I built a new dream in my mind in honor of my brother. I told myself that I would build a "Dosan University" in honor of Dosan and Young-ik in Pyongyang when Korea unified as one again. I want "One nation, indivisible" for Korea and I want it soon so that I can build my brother's university in Pyongyang before I die.

So I refocused my energy to the positive, since negative energy is so exhausting. The university idea was fresh on my mind when Yenzi University invited me to speak at the school, and I gladly accepted the invitation.

Out of the roughly two million Koreans living in China, about 600,000 Koreans live in the Yenzi region, a unique region with its own autonomy in the eastern end of Manchuria. Many centuries ago, the region had belonged to Korea, and the Korean presence there is as ancient as history. The university people had heard about me through the newspapers and television coverage in South Korea as well as my book that was written in Korean. One of the professors had seen the book in Seoul. It drew his interest because I was an engineer, and he brought it back to Yenzi and shared it with his colleagues. They wrote to me and asked me for the permission to translate it into Chinese for the students. I wrote back to them and gave them my permission along with 1,000 copies of the book. Soon after, they invited me to Yenzi to address the student body.

Sue and I went to Seoul in May 2002 and caught a flight to Yenzi, two hours away from Seoul by airplane. To our surprise, the Vice Chancellor of the University and the Party Secretary of Yenzi greeted us at the airport, and a girl in a beautiful Korean costume gave us flowers. An army of reporters and cameramen swarmed around us, making me wonder if they were expecting someone else. Surely, the red carpet reception was meant for a statesman or something, we said, as they led us to a Mercedes Benz limousine with a police escort. The police motorcade went ahead of us with their lights blinking, and our limousine followed them, then another car carrying the staff. As we drove towards downtown, we noted that all the street signs and store signs were in Korean with Chinese subscripts, to which the Vice Chancellor explained matter-of-factly, "Korean is the official language in Yenzi."

We marveled, "That's wonderful!"

The Vice Chancellor smiled and nodded, "Our children grow up learning Korean and Chinese. They are proficient in both languages."

"That's wonderful," I repeated, "to learn both languages because they want to, without being forced to."

"Yes, it is natural for them to speak Korean at home and at school. Korean is the official language here so there's no pressure to learn Chinese. But they speak, read and write Chinese because they want to. They're comfortable with the duality, being Koreans with Chinese passports."

I was stunned that such a bi-lingual region could exist harmoniously without oppression or resentment. I told him that in my own case, I spoke Korean at home and Japanese in school as a youngster. It wasn't because I had an option. I had to speak Japanese in school because if I spoke Korean at school I was punished. I spoke Korean at home, of course. I didn't dare speak Japanese at home because my father would have whipped me if I was caught speaking Japanese. I was actually ashamed that I could speak and write Japanese. When the liberation came at the end of World War II, I spoke Korean at school, and no Japanese. I slipped up a few times and spoke Japanese to Korean teachers because we were conditioned to speak Japanese at school. Each time I made the mistake of speaking Japanese, the Korean teachers and classmates made fun of me, and I made fun of others who made the same mistake.

In Yenzi, the youngsters speak Korean or Chinese freely, reading books and newspapers in either language, and watching Chinese TV programs as well as the Korean TV programs coming out of Seoul.

"They're fortunate," was all I could say to the Vice Chancellor.

"They think that's the way it should be, and they don't

know any other way," the Vice Chancellor said, and I came to a new realization that the days of fear tactics were over. I felt good about the future for Yenzi as the motorcade moved into the downtown area.

We stopped in front of Dae Woo Hotel, our home for three nights and four days. After we checked into the new, big suite and washed up, the driver drove us to the university. To our surprise, a huge sign hung above the main gate, "Welcome, Mr. and Mrs. Paik." The President of the University was waiting for us, and I liked Mr. Kim Jin-Kyung immediately. He gave us a tour around the campus with a student population of about 2,000 and the faculty of about 200. All of the students were on scholarship with free room and board because they came from poor families, and 99 percent of the students were Korean, and one percent Chinese. Mr. Kim was very proud of the bright student body, boys and girls, who were all eager to make something of themselves in life. "They're high achievers, and their families expect a lot from them. They like the school so much that they stay here on weekends and during vacation. Also, they don't go home because they don't have much to eat at home. They don't want to take the food that would otherwise go to other family members."

After the tour of the big and meticulous campus nestled in the hillside overlooking the entire city, Mr. Kim guided us to the nearby city called Yongjung. Yongjung is known for the independence workers during the Japanese rule over Korea, and is also a home for many writers and poets like Yoon Dong-Ju, Ahn Su-Gil, and Richard Kim. We went to Dae Sung School, where the town had honored Yoon Dong-Ju, the brilliant poet, with a bronze statue.

We came back to Yenzi and Mr. Kim took us out to dinner at a restaurant, where they cooked and served *bulgogi*, the marinated beef strips, on red-hot stones that are found only in the legendary Kumkang Mountains. The northern cuisine was delicious, with the fresh vegetables from Baekdu Mountains, and we enjoyed the meal in leisure.

Next morning after coffee with the Party Secretary of the University, he took us on a tour to Tohmun, a border town on the Tumen River about 30 km away. It had a bridge that connected North Korea and China. The shallow river was narrow, taking up only the middle third of the bridge span. The Party Secretary explained to us that one-half of the Tohmun Bridge belonged to China, and the other half to North Korea. I saw that the Chinese side was well developed with high-rise apartment buildings, its streets busy with cars, shops, and shoppers. A lone guard played with children, and when he wasn't playing with the children, he took pictures for tourists.

On the other hand, the North Korean side was quiet and eerily still. North Korean border guards stood prominently while a few people walked slowly or were sitting down doing nothing. An old coal-burning train puffed a string of smoke as it chugged along the river slowly.

A short bridge set the two worlds apart like night and day, and it made very little sense that there was no traffic on the bridge. *How odd,* I thought. *The bridge should be busy with people going back and forth, but it is not. On the prosperous side, the lone guard plays with children. On the poor side, the soldiers look as though they're ready to shoot anyone who crosses the bridge. Why is Pyongyang so damn stubborn? Can't they see what's going on here?*

I was sad and puzzled, and I posed the question to my host, but he didn't have an answer. He said, "Many people here think that Pyongyang leadership is bad. They give no food to the people. But the people still have to keep working without seeing any result. They have nothing to work for over there."

The bridge was quite a revelation for me, and I thought

about what I was going to say to the students on the way back to the University.

I saw pride on the faces of the Korean Chinese students when I began my speech in the auditorium. They looked bright and eager like the University President had said, and I opened with my days as a refugee, begging for and stealing food sometimes. You could have heard the proverbial pin drop in the large auditorium. I said, "I used to feel ashamed to beg for food in those days, but now I know that people have the right to eat."

Coming from their own poor backgrounds, the students immediately understood what I was talking about. They agreed with me wholeheartedly, applauding loudly for quite a while.

I continued, "As a Korean American addressing the Korean Chinese people, I think we share the same goal of bettering our lives and building a successful life for ourselves and our family. I want to share some things I learned in my life, hoping that you will benefit by my experiences. In America, I began with no money, no English. But I never thought of giving up. I had an idea, to get an education, and I stayed with it until I got it. Looking back, it was a hard struggle, I suppose. But in those days, I didn't think of it as a hard struggle. It was just a matter of doing what was necessary to survive. I knew that education was the way out of poverty, and I stayed focused on my goal. That way, nothing was hard..."

"You are already here in this fine institution and you're well on your way to achieving your goal. You have taken the step to improve your life and the lives around you, and I can see a promising future in front of you. As an engineer I looked for better ways, more economic ways, and new ways to do things. As a businessman, I looked for the ways to make things easier and better for my customers. Be true to yourself and your ideas. Be true to others. Honesty and integrity are your tools to successful life. Stay focused on your ideas and never, never give up."

The speech went over well, I thought. I could see the excitement in their eyes as they came up to me afterwards, asking me to sign their copies of the book that I had donated to the school. I stayed over an hour to sign the books and I felt confident that the young people would play a major role in Yenzi's future. I hoped that I'd done something to help the young people.

The evening schedule took us to the City Hall for the Mayor's reception. All the officials were lined up at the entrance and greeted me as we walked up the red carpet. Once again, the press swarmed all around us as we walked to the banquet hall. In the stately banquet hall, there were five large tables adorned with flowers, and we sat at the center table with Mayor Cha Jong-Il, University President Kim Jin-Kyung, Mrs. Kim, the Party Secretary from the City and the University, Sue, and myself. Everyone settled in at the respective tables, and Mayor Cha stood up and made gracious welcoming remarks. As graciously as I could, I thanked the City in return for the warm welcome, a reception fit for a homecoming hero.

So began the banquet, with exquisite dishes flowing as freely as the conversation at the table. Naturally, the conversation centered on the topic of economy. They were very interested in learning from the U.S. and South Korea, the various types of economic engines that had propelled them to the economic powers.

In broad terms, I told them that the American infrastructure played a huge role in building up the economy, and they perked up. "We want to do that. We want to build up our infrastructure. Mr. Paik, please come and visit us often and be our economic advisor."

"Yes, I would like to," I said, "I want to see a world-class infrastructure here to attract many industries."

The Party Secretary said, "We revised our view on building up industries. The Party has taken a position to help the industry rather than trying to control it. In the capitalist economy, the government doesn't interfere with private companies, as I understand it."

"That's correct. The government leaves them alone. It doesn't tell them what to make, how much to produce, what to charge, and so forth. Over here, too, the government should take out 40 or 50-year loans from the World Bank and build highways, bring power, gas and water, and improve them continually. Industries will come. For instance, in Palm Springs, California, they transformed a desert to a golfer's paradise. There was no water, so they brought in water. They use wind power for electricity. Golf is a big industry in America. Tiger Woods had a tremendous impact on improving the industry. Ten years ago, kids didn't play golf. Now five-year-old children learn to play golf."

Mayor Cha smiled and said, "Today, I approved a South Korean company for a golf course. I did the right thing, I see."

We clapped and laughed, "Yes, you did the right thing, absolutely." And I added, "Well, you don't have to worry about bringing in water. You have plenty of water around here."

"Yes, we have water, electricity, and gas. Plus good labor force. The Party manages the free food and free housing program for the labor force, and the labor is willing to sacrifice on the wages. We have no labor problem."

"So, eating and sleeping is taken care of for everybody?"

"Yes. That's a little different from the traditional Chinese philosophy. Historically, the Chinese thinking is that everyone takes care of his own life's needs. In that sense, the market economy fits the Chinese character better. But we think that our labor system frees the workers from worrying about the basic things."

"How wonderful," I said, thinking about my hungry days. I wondered if there were problems in managing such a system for the huge population, but I didn't ask the Party Secretary how well it worked. North Korea has a similar system, but it hadn't worked for many years, evidenced by the starving population there. There was no point in bringing up the North Korean neighbors to the south. The evening belonged to Yenzi and Yenzi alone, and its bright future. Their enthusiasm was contagious, and I felt a special kinship with my fellow Koreans living in China, who had to overcome years of hunger and hardship of their own. They were well on their way to prosperity now, using the phrase "market economy," the most popular phrase at the dinner table, and I don't recall hearing the word "communism" any time during dinner. To my surprise, they talked openly about the Party's control mechanism, and its negative impact. "We are skeptical about the Party control, and the policies now reflect such skepticism."

In between these lively conversations everyone took turns to tell me, "Please come back soon," and they didn't stop until I promised that I would.

Next morning we got up early. It was the day to visit the legendary Baekdu Mountains about three hours away by car. After the quick breakfast we piled into a Toyota with a 4-wheel-drive and headed west to the mountains where Dahn Gun had descended from the heavens to establish the ancient Chosun nation in 2333BC. The ride was very pleasant, and I enjoyed the beautiful scenery with its sprawling farms along the way. The guide told us that all of Baekdu Mountains used to belong to North Korea before the Korean War in 1950. After the war, the border was redrawn between North Korea and China through the volcanic lake at the top of the grand mountain. We were on our way to the mountains from the Chinese side, and my heart quickened as the mountains loomed in the distance. I was about to see Baekdu Mountains for the first time in my life, the Baekdu Mountains that I had sung about in the Korean anthem ever since I was a child. "Baek" stands for whiteness, and "Du" means head, and I saw why it was called Baekdu, with the ever-present white cloud hovering over its peak.

We stopped in a restaurant for lunch and after lunch the guide took us to Baekdu waterfall. It was cold and windy there, and we rented Chinese army jackets for two dollars each. The jackets kept us from freezing as we admired the waterfall and the magnificent view of the mountain up ahead. I don't remember how long we stood out in the cold, and when the guide asked us if we wanted to try the hot spring, we all said, yes. Baekdu Hotel was built around the natural hot spring, and the spring water is said to be hot enough to boil an egg. They mix cold water to cool it down enough for people to withstand the heat, the guide said, but the water was still very hot in the tub, and I forgot about the cold wind at the waterfall. It was the best hot tub I have ever been in. I felt like a new man and I was ready to go up to the peak to see the lake that had inspired so many poets and thinkers. The car went up and down the steep, icy two-lane road. The driver guided the 4-wheel drive vehicle very carefully over the slippery road. He parked the car and I followed the guide over the snowy ground for about 150 yards. The wind was very strong and cold. It was overcast but clear, and when I finally came up to the blue sapphire body of water in front of me, I gasped. The lake was two and quarter miles in diameter, not a huge one, but its depth of over nine hundred feet gave it the deep and mystical color that seemed beyond this world. I looked across the lake and stared at the stillness on the North Korean side of Chun Ji, heavenly body of water, and I said a quiet prayer, "Rest in peace, Young-ik. Rest in peace, mother."

We took some pictures, and we descended the mountain on the same road that we had come up, leaving the wintry cold wind behind and entering the warmth of early summer. Back in Yenzi, we went to a leisurely dinner hosted by the professors from the university, sharing our trip to Baekdu Mountains and the myriad vegetable dishes that the ancient poets and scholars might have enjoyed. I was surrounded by modern day scholars who had come to Yenzi University to donate their time and wisdom for the young and hungry. The professors had come from the U.S. and South Korea to feed the hungry minds in return for room and board and for the satisfaction that their students would do the same for another generation, and another generation. They reminded me of the kind professors I had met in Busan, Seoul, Eugene, and Fort Wayne, who helped me shape my life along the way.

I felt hope. With people like these around, I felt that there was hope for North Korea as well. Without hope there is no future, and the future belongs to the young, in Yenzi and the other side of Tohmun Bridge and beyond. It is up to us, the older generation, to feed hope to the young so that they can dream about a better world for themselves and for others, a world without deceit, a world without fear.

Yes, the days of nurturing fear are over. I saw a future in Yenzi. I saw it in their young, bright eyes. I thought, it is time to work on the fear of hunger in North Korea and put an end to the lies. The proof is in Tohmun at the bridge to oblivion. The old guards must step aside, and open the bridge for goodwill and hope to come through, to feed the starved youth and nurture their dreams for a better world.

EPILOG

Recently, out of the blue, a letter came from North Korea. Supposedly, it was written by my brother Young-su, the younger of the two brothers. Young-su and Young-ik were both dead as far as I was concerned, or anyone else for that matter. A man named P.J. Choi sent it, claiming that he had found Young-su. He sent a photograph along with the letter and a few seconds worth of videotape.

February 6, 2004
To My Big Brother,
How have you been, my big brother?
I just heard that you were alive, and I don't
know whether I should believe it or not...
It's hard to accept the news. They tell me that
they will send this letter to you. I can't imagine
how this can be possible.
How is your family?
I am fine and healthy.
What I remember most about you is the time

when you went to Pyongyang for the speech

contest during your middle school days.

You won the first prize and you brought back a

nickel coated bookmark. The whole family

was very happy and proud of you.

Also, I can't forget the times you'd come home

once in a while, and mother would cook the fish

that Young-ik and I had caught together at the river.

You used to pat me on the back and say that I was

the best.

I have so many things to say and write, but time

is limited. Besides, I can't write any more because

the tears come before the words.

They tell me that I'll be able to see you some day,

and that would be so wonderful if it is true.

What are you doing, where are you, I really want to

see you. I am 66 years old already, which makes you 74.

I wonder if I can see you before I die, if I really

get to see you. My wish is that I see you once before

I die.

Whatever you may be doing, please work hard for the unification of our fatherland.

I sincerely wish good health and happiness for you and your family.

Your kid brother, Young-su

Needless to say, the letter bowled me over. I read the letter over and over, incredulous that I was holding a letter that had actually come from Young-su, who was presumed dead. He was the one who had complained to the authorities for imprisoning the other brother Young-ik under the trumped-up charges. The North Korean authorities hadn't taken his complaint too kindly, and they sent him off to a concentration camp.

The old memory of Young-su flooded in with new tears that I didn't know I had left in me. I looked at his latest photograph that came with the letter. He was standing in front of a wall wearing a fuzzy Russian style hat, and I presumed that the photograph was taken inside the camp. He was twelve and I was twenty years old when I saw him last fifty-fours years ago. The resemblance was there, however, and I said, yes, that's him. Next instant, I told myself, no, that can't be him. Mother had said that he was dead. I'm thinking that this man in the picture is my brother because I want to believe that he is alive. I can't trust my own memory, I must be careful of what I see, what I remember. But then he is talking about the fish, the small fish that mother used to marinate in soy sauce and fry in the pan just for me and no one else. And he is talking about the speech contest in Pyongyang. No one outside of the family can remember this. But then he is talking about a nickel-plated bookmark. I never brought home a prize, they never gave me any prize, but where did the bookmark come from? His memory may be hazy. Maybe he made it up. Why would he make up something like that, though?

Oh, how I wanted to see him right then and ask him all

these questions. He wrote that he hadn't known that I was alive. How can that be? I was in Pyongyang fifteen years ago, met my mother, my sister, and my nephews and nieces, then again a few years later before mother passed away. Apparently, Young-su never got the news about me. He presumed that I was dead all along. Mother couldn't tell him; she thought he was dead.

He said he wanted to see me before he died, and I wanted to fly over there right then, but I shook off the thought immediately. When I was there last time, the Party officials had tried to wrangle a million dollars out of me, telling me that they were going to find my brothers for me. They badgered me all night until I signed a piece of paper that said, "I will do my best as far as the U.S. laws would allow." Nothing had come out of that fiasco, and now, they were coming back at me with Young-su's letter, picture, and a few frames of faint videotape. Yes, these material were a fair indication that he was still alive somewhere. But I wasn't sure when the picture was taken, or when the letter was written.

When P.J. Choi called from a Chinese border town—across the river from North Korea—I told him, "There will be no money until you bring him out to China."

He insisted that Young-su was alive and that I believe him. I told him that I wanted to believe him, but I had to be sure. "Bring him out," I said, "then we'll talk."

That wasn't the reaction he was looking for, but I wasn't about to commit myself to what could be a ploy to extract money from me. Money was what they wanted, and Mr. Choi was not calling me and sending me things all the way from China out of the goodness of his heart. I had been down that road before, and mere words wouldn't do it for me.

What Choi said next stunned me. He said, "Young-ik is alive," meaning the older one of the two.

Young-ik? I hollered, "Did you say Young-ik?"

He said, "Yes."

I was speechless. Finally I said, "Don't lie to me. Don't

play with my emotions. We're talking about people's lives here!"

He replied, "If you don't believe me, I'll let you talk to someone here. He's an important person from the Central Party."

Choi switched me over to the man whose name I can't recall now. The Party man said, "Yes, it's true. Young-ik is alive. He's in the political prison. We'll send you his photograph and video. Will you come and see him?"

I remained silent for a long time. I heard the telephone crackle thousands of miles away. Finally, I said, "Bring both of them out to China, and we'll talk."

So it began again, my journey into the world of oblivion and my life-long quest for a moment with Young-ik. One hug, one hello would have dispelled the dark cloud that haunted me ever since I left him in the woodsy hill behind the old house. The look of disappointment on his adolescent face... the way he turned around with his head down... his bare feet dragging on the ground towards home... stopping and turning around to see if I changed my mind about taking him with me... the look of hope, then my refusal, disappointment again, and final submission to disappointment... These images came back to me like lightning.

It had taken me a long time to accept the fact that Young-ik was gone, and now, they were telling me that he was alive, too. None of these things made sense, my EOY award in the world's richest country in contrast to my brothers' demise in the poor country that is battling the harshest famine known to mankind; that brothers from one family should travel in such contradictory paths.

The North Korean powers-that-be didn't know who my brothers were, who I was, until they saw the potential dollars from me. They are orchestrating a charade to extort a million dollars, which I would be glad to part with provided that they produce my brothers. I would help them with General Motors even if I have to drag the automobile giant in there with my own bare hands, plus more.

I have said it and I say again, all I want is to see my brothers. At the bottom of my mission is to see my brothers, and only that. I want the North Korean officials to appreciate the simple truth in that statement and I pray to God that they would understand me some day. But I am not holding my breath waiting for them to come around. I've waited over half a century to know the truth about my brothers, and I have no reason to believe that things are different now. When I see my brothers, touch them, hug them in my arms, and talk freely—away from the eyes and ears of the secret police—I'll know the truth then, not before. In the meantime, I dream and pray that someday soon brothers and sisters can come and go freely across North and South Korea.